HUMMUS BROS

LEVANTINE
KITCHEN

HUMMUS BROS

LEVANTINE KITCHEN

Photography by
Karen Thomas

PAVILION

RECIPES
INSPIRED BY
THE **ANCIENT**
MEDITERRANEAN,
SERVED
WITHOUT CEREMONY
—CUTLERY
OPTIONAL.

CONTENTS

HUMMUS FOR THE PEOPLE

6

HUMMUS BROS WAS BORN ON A GLORIOUS HOT DAY IN MAY 2003, WHEN, AS TWO COLLEGE FRIENDS, WE WERE SEARCHING FOR SOMETHING FILLING AND HEALTHY THAT WOULD TASTE GREAT, AND STILL LEAVE SOME CHANGE FOR DRINKS AT THE UNION BAR. Passing on the usual options of pizza or sandwiches, we stumbled out of a small delicatessen with three basic ingredients: pitta bread, hummus and olive oil. In no time at all, the bowls of hummus were wiped spotlessly clean. 'I could eat a good meal like that every day!' someone remarked. We looked at each other and smiled – a dream was born: to open a place dedicated to hummus.

Having our own place, where hummus could be served and celebrated with imaginative flair, was our one overriding ambition from that day on. We spent every spare moment in our small kitchen – cooking, mixing and caressing chickpeas to get that perfect combination of texture and taste. Weekends or weekdays, before or after lectures – we just had to get it right. Little did we know how challenging it would be, but after months of experimenting with different ingredients, countless tasting sessions and facing public scrutiny in busy markets, we finally got there. The recipe was a winner.

Now it was time to take Hummus Bros to the people...

THE FIRST HUMMUS BROS

TWO YEARS LATER, IN AUGUST 2005, THE FIRST HUMMUS BROS OPENED ON WARDOUR STREET, SOHO. IT WAS RECEIVED TO CRITICAL ACCLAIM AND WE SOON OPENED OUR SECOND BRANCH IN HOLBORN IN JANUARY 2007. WE NOW RUN FOUR POPULAR BRANCHES ACROSS LONDON.

Our superior tasting hummus is made daily from carefully selected, fresh ingredients. We serve it with mouth-watering toppings and beautifully warm pitta bread. A unique selection of salads, soups, desserts and coffee complements the feast.

Inspired taste, value for money and quality of service is how sophisticated marketing people might describe our offer, but for us, it's simpler than that: it's about making great hummus.

Now, we want to bring it into your home through this book. You will find recipes that everyone in the family can enjoy – from children (the simple garlic-free hummus is often a winner) to adults, and from meat-eaters to vegans. This book is for everyone who wants to eat healthy, filling and delicious food that is easy to make (we don't do complicated food).

Hummus can be eaten as a dip, a main course or as a side dish. So whether you are looking to make a hearty dish for a cold winter evening (Hummus with Chunky Beef on p.35, for example), make a salad for a picnic (the tabouleh is yummy and zingy) or a light snack/dip (our hummus or falafels are particularly suited for this) we hope you will find a recipe for the occasion.

ABOUT US

CONTRARY TO POPULAR BELIEF, WE ARE NOT BROTHERS. HERE'S A BIT ABOUT US TO HELP YOU UNDERSTAND OUR LOVE AFFAIR WITH CHICKPEAS.

RONEN

I was born and raised in Israel on a kibbutz. I used to hate the food that was served to everyone in the large communal dining hall and subsequently was a very fussy eater until my teens. However, from around the age of 16, hummus became my obsession – a food to eat with friends on Saturday afternoons and after evenings out (I still associate it with that 2 a.m. feeling: plastic furniture on the pavement of Tel Aviv, cars driving past and honking). This was our fast food; we didn't eat burgers. It was cheap and accessible.

We used to sit in different hummus places in Tel Aviv and discuss which one was cleaner, tastier, grainier, came with better falafel, and which owner was opening which shop and which one was fatter because he ate too much bread. We followed the rise and fall of each place as if it were our own, curious when a new shop opened up (because the chef from the guy across the street left and opened his own place), and sad to see a good place closing because the guy emigrated to Australia. Each one of my friends had their preferred hummus restaurant and frowned upon others' choices (if the meet up was scheduled in a place that was not my favourite I used to complain).

It was as much about the atmosphere that came with the hummus as the food itself that made a place worthy of a visit. To this day it has a social meaning for me. It's food to share with friends, to laugh over and love.

The hummus commonly sold in supermarkets has developed out of Cypriot/Turkish origins, when it became popular in the 70s. I prefer the Lebanese/Israeli type, of course, which is smoother and uses less garlic (if at all), but that's because of where I come from. Hummus is a very sensitive product and deteriorates in quality very quickly if freshly made, so supermarket stuff is full of preservatives to give it a month's shelf life. It is healthier to make your own and it will taste so much better, but making hummus takes some practice – it won't come out right the first time, so be ready for that.

For me, the best meal of the week is weekend brunch – I make Shakshuka (see p.48) for the whole family and my friends with a host of other dishes (which are all found in this book). I get up early with my daughter and we cook for three hours. Shakshuka is such a social dish. Try putting a pot of hummus on the table when you make it and you will see it's really a match made in heaven. All my friends keep wanting to be invited over to have it.

Hummus is such simple cuisine and so easy to fall in love with. It's colourful and fresh and so unassuming. You can bastardise it as you wish – we did! If anyone in the Middle East heard that we serve hummus with guacamole they'd think it was criminal. I'm sure there will be a debate by the hardcore hummus consumers about what we do/don't do right, but mainly we want people to look at our food and say 'I wanna make that'.

CHRISTIAN

I am half French/half English. When my family comes together at weekends, we eat my mother's or grandmother's cooking, which will often be Mediterranean-inspired dishes such as tabouleh, spaghetti Bolognese, salade Niçoise...and it inspired my love of food from all over the world.

I hadn't eaten hummus at all until I went to university, when I started eating hummus with whatever else was in the fridge and soon realised that it could go with anything. The food we serve at Hummus Bros is predominantly from the Levantine region with an element of this fusion – we serve our hummus with dishes from Mexico, India, Thailand...

We're not accomplished chefs – we don't have a big experimental kitchen! If we taste something good, we try to recreate it as simply as possible, so that it's easy for our chefs to make and always get right. Hopefully this will encourage you to try some of these recipes from two people who knew next to nothing about food or restaurants just 9 years ago and who now serve thousands of people every day.

My favourite recipes are Hummus with Chunky Beef (see p.34) – the beef is slow cooked so it is very tender and goes beautifully with the hummus – and the Falafel Salad on p.89 with the crunchy cabbage, tzatziki, tomato salsa and crispy falafel is another winner. The bread you use to scoop up your hummus is also very important. I urge you to try our homemade recipe for this (see p.110) – it will transform the way you look at hummus forever.

THE LEVANTINE KITCHEN

THE TERM 'LEVANT' FIRST APPEARED IN ENGLISH IN 1497, AND
ORIGINALLY MEANT THE EAST IN GENERAL OR 'MEDITERRANEAN
LANDS EAST OF ITALY.' IT IS BORROWED FROM THE FRENCH
LEVANT OR 'RISING', THAT IS, THE PLACE WHERE THE SUN RISES.
AT A TIME WHEN THE MEDITERRANEAN WAS THE CENTRE OF
THE KNOWN WORLD, THE LEVANT REFERRED TO THE EASTERN
MEDITERRANEAN, LITERALLY WHERE THE SUN ROSE.

As a geographic and cultural region, the Levant consists of the 'eastern
Mediterranean littoral between Anatolia and Egypt' and can be said to
encompass Cyprus, Lebanon, Syria, the Palestinian territories, Jordan,
Israel, part of southern Turkey, and the Aleppo Vilayet.

Perhaps the most distinctive aspects of Levantine cuisine are mezze
dishes, including hummus, tabouleh, falafel and baba ghanoush.
Chickpeas and tahini (a paste of crushed sesame seeds) feature
heavily. But the nature of the area and its significance as a meeting
point of trading routes, means that flavours from all over the world
have often come together in its food.

Our Levantine style of hummus is smooth and not flavoured with
garlic at all. This means it can accept other strong flavours well.
Given how versatile hummus is, we have expanded on this cuisine
to include many dishes from various countries and cultures, such as
chicken tikka or lamb rogan josh from India, guacamole from Mexico,
a sausage casserole from Eastern Europe...

Our food is nothing new – it's been done before a million times,
but we simplify it to the bare minimum to extract clear, fresh flavours.
The tabouleh is lemony, the fava is earthy and the hummus is smooth
and very moreish.

INGREDIENTS

WHAT ATTRACTED US TO HUMMUS WHEN WE WERE AT COLLEGE WAS HOW EASY IT IS TO MAKE AND EAT WITH WHATEVER FOOD YOU ARE HAVING. JUST SOME CHICKPEAS, A SPOONFUL OF TAHINI, LEMON JUICE, A PINCH OF SALT AND YOU HAVE GOT THE MAKINGS OF LUNCH. IT IS HEALTHY AND FILLING, AND VEGETARIANS, VEGANS AND MEAT-EATERS, AS WELL AS PEOPLE WITH MOST FOOD INTOLERANCES, CAN ALL EAT IT.

DESPITE ITS POPULARITY, VERY FEW PEOPLE ACTUALLY MAKE THEIR OWN HUMMUS. WHICH IS A SHAME, BECAUSE FRESH HUMMUS IS A WORLD AWAY FROM THE SUPERMARKET SOUR SLURRY, SEASONED WITH PRESERVATIVES, AND SOLID ENOUGH TO RE-TILE THE BATHROOM, AND HALF THE PRICE, TOO. MAKE IT WITH TOP-NOTCH FRESH INGREDIENTS AND IT WILL BLOW YOU AWAY.

CHICKPEAS IN OUR TIME: CANNED VS DRIED

At Hummus Bros we make hummus from dried chickpeas that we soak for 12 hours before cooking them. If you are in a rush you can use canned chickpeas, although we don't recommend it! The dried chickpeas definitely have a nuttier flavour, and they also give the hummus a grainier texture. Many brands of canned chickpeas are crunchy and undercooked; however, you can now buy jars of excellent ready-cooked chickpeas, preserved in water and salt, without added artificial preservatives.

SECRET (SOFTENING) AGENTS

We cook our chickpeas with bicarbonate of soda to make sure that they are soft enough to make creamy hummus. This prevents the calcium in our London tap water from cementing together the pectin molecules in the pea's cell walls – in fact, the alkaline water that it produces actively encourages these pectins to separate, creating a softening effect.

We use 10g/¼oz bicarbonate of soda per 500g/1lb 2oz dried chickpeas. After a 12-hour soaking period, the chickpeas take a quarter of the time to cook – and achieve that lovely fluffy texture which makes such great hummus.

Too much bicarbonate of soda can give the chickpeas an unpleasant soapy quality, so always err on the side of caution. This also robs them of much of their nutritional value.

THE SKIN OF THE CHICKPEAS

Most people are surprised to find out that chickpeas have a skin. During our research into making the best hummus we were often told that peeling chickpeas gave a superior colour and flavour to the end product. The skin is actually easy to remove, once the chickpeas are cooked; although given the size of the things, it's a tough task! In our experiments we felt that it was better to keep the skins on and add them, along with the water in which the chickpeas were cooked, to make the hummus 'mother' recipe (see p.19).

OLIVE OIL

Customers often ask if we use olive oil in our hummus! The only oil we use is tahini, which is made from crushed sesame seeds (see below). We do add a drizzle of olive oil to chickpea and fava bean toppings, but none in the hummus itself!

TAHINI

Tahini is the very essence of the flavours of the Levantine kitchen, and the basis for tahini sauce and hummus (it's too thick to eat on its own). The word 'tahini' comes from the Hebrew/Arabic root of the word 'to grind'. It is made from 100 per cent sesame seeds, sometimes with a small amount of salt added (typically 0.4 per cent in our tahini).

The sesame seeds are cleaned, hulled and roasted, then ground several times to make the paste we know as tahini.

Different colours of tahini originate either from the type of seed used, or, more commonly, from the level of roasting. Naturally, the longer the seeds are roasted, the darker the tahini. If the tahini is particularly white, it is possible that the manufacturer used a chemical hulling process with caustic soda, which bleaches the seeds somewhat. It might look good, but it isn't great in terms of nutrition! Some tahini manufacturers have recently started making 'whole tahini', which involves hulling, roasting the seeds and then adding the shells to the mixture which is ground (the shells are not roasted). This results in tahini with a higher calcium content. However, most tahini used in hummus today does not contain the shells.

Look for tahini made with organic 'Humera' sesame seeds, usually grown in Ethiopia, and sometimes Paraguay. Some inferior tahini is made from Nigerian seeds, but we only buy tahini with Humera seeds for our restaurant.

Our tahini is not particularly white or dark; it is hulled and tastes slightly salty and almost sweet. It is also quite thick whereas a lot of the tahini sold on the market is watery. The ultimate test for tahini is to taste it pure, without any addition of water. If there is an aftertaste (which is usually bitter), then this will certainly come out in the taste of the finished hummus. When you have high-quality tahini made from the right seeds there is no aftertaste and the consistency is almost quicksand-like, which sticks to the top of your mouth. If you can easily eat a spoonful of raw tahini that means it's not good enough.

GARLIC?

The balance of garlic and lemon juice is very personal and this is why in the restaurant we let customers add as much or as little as they want, by putting it on the tables as a condiment. We feel that hummus should taste of chickpeas and tahini.

HOW TO TOP IT

Hummus is, of course, ideal dipping material, but it can be dressed up into a proper meal. Over the past nine years we have experimented with the best toppings. From the traditional toppings of boiled chickpeas or fava (broad/ful medames) beans with a hard-boiled egg to vegetarian toppings, such as Vegetable Salad (p.88) or Falafel Salad (p.89), and meat toppings such as beef stew (p.35) or Lamb Rogan Josh (p.38).

HEALTHY HUMMUS

1 HEALTH BENEFITS OF CHICKPEAS
Chickpeas are very healthy because they do not contain any cholesterol or saturated fats. They are also rich in protein. This makes hummus a favourite among vegetarians. A fantastic source of slow-release energy, chickpeas are also known to be effective in preventing the build up of cholesterol in blood vessels and can help maintain correct blood sugar levels.

2 NUTRITIONAL VALUE OF TAHINI
Tahini, meanwhile, is full of fat and calories. However, the fact that it is used sparingly in most hummus recipes and that it mostly contains unsaturated fat means there is not much to worry about. Tahini is also high in protein and is a great source of valuable calcium.

**3 OPTIONAL ADDITIONS:
GARLIC, LEMON JUICE, OLIVE OIL**
Another healthy ingredient often found alongside hummus is olive oil. As most people know, olive oil is a healthy fat, as it has a high monounsaturated fat content but is low in saturated fat. This oil can help regulate cholesterol and protect the heart from various diseases. Garlic and lemon juice, meanwhile, are filled with antioxidants that reduce oxidative stress in the body. They also work to improve immune functions and the fight of bacteria and viruses. And, of course, lemon juice is full of vitamin C.

4 GENERAL HEALTH BENEFITS OF HUMMUS
Hummus as a whole contains plenty of omega 3 fatty acids, which are great for improving intelligence and maintaining a healthy heart. On top of it all, this dish also has iron, vitamin B6, manganese, copper, folic acid and amino acids. Tryptophan, phenylalanine and tyrosine are the amino acids found in hummus that can promote good-quality sleep and uplift one's mood.

HUMMUS IS LOADED WITH NUTRIENTS THAT CAN CONTRIBUTE TO A HEALTHY LIFESTYLE. INCLUDE IT IN YOUR DIET BY USING IT AS A SPREAD ON SANDWICHES AND WRAPS, AS A BASE FOR YOUR SALAD, AS A DIP FOR RAW VEGETABLES, OR AS A SIDE DISH FOR MAIN COURSES.

MAKING HUMMUS

BASIC HUMMUS RECIPE

SERVES: 16–20
MAKES: 1.8KG/4LB
PREP: 15 MINUTES
SOAK: 12 HOURS,
OR OVERNIGHT
COOK: 1–1½ HOURS

DON'T BE DECEIVED, THOUGH THE SIMPLEST OF PROCESSES, MAKING HUMMUS IS AN ART FORM. IT TAKES PRACTICE TO GET IT JUST RIGHT, BUT ONCE YOU DO THE REWARDS ARE HUGE.

OK, SO YOU NEED TO REMEMBER TO SOAK THE CHICKPEAS THE DAY BEFORE BUT THERE REALLY IS VERY LITTLE INVOLVED WITH SOAKING OR COOKING THEM.

ALL THE INGREDIENTS ARE PRETTY INEXPENSIVE, BUT THAT SAID, DO TRY TO FIND THE BEST TAHINI (SESAME PASTE), AS YOUR HUMMUS WILL TASTE SO MUCH BETTER.

THE FOLLOWING RECIPE IS FOR QUITE A LARGE QUANTITY, BUT IT STORES WELL FOR UP TO THREE DAYS IN THE FRIDGE AND IT'S QUICKLY EATEN BY THE AVERAGE HOUSEHOLD. IF YOU LIKE, THE RECIPE IS EASILY HALVED.

SEE OVERLEAF FOR METHOD.

1 Tip the chickpeas into a bowl and cover with plenty of cold water (they will expand as they soak). Cover and leave to soak – there's no need to refrigerate them – for 12 hours, or overnight. There aren't any shortcuts to this, just aim to put them to soak the day before you need them.

2 Drain the chickpeas and put into a medium saucepan. Pour in the fresh measured cold water so that the water only covers the chickpeas by about 2cm (¾in). Stir in the bicarbonate of soda, then bring the water to the boil. Don't be tempted to add salt at this stage as it can make the chickpeas tough. Keep a watchful eye as it comes to the boil as it can easily boil over.

3 Skim off scum, if liked, with a slotted spoon. Cook over a medium heat for 1–1½ hours until the chickpeas are very soft. If the water level seems to be going down too quickly then partially cover the pan with a lid to help reduce evaporation, but don't cover the top completely or the pan will boil over. Keep an eye on the water level and top up with a little extra boiling water from the kettle if needed,

especially towards the end of cooking. Stir from time to time, stirring more towards the end of cooking, as the chickpeas take on a soupy texture as there is less water in the pan.

4 Once cooked, drain the liquid if there is a lot, but don't throw it away – keep it for later to adjust the consistency. Spread the chickpeas over the surface of a large roasting tin and leave to cool.

5 You should have about 1.25kg/2lb 7oz cooked chickpeas. Purée in batches with any liquid from the roasting tin in a food processor, adding the tahini, lemon juice and salt to taste until you have a creamy, velvety smooth consistency. Adjust the consistency with some of the reserved cooking liquid or water. You may need to do this in batches depending on the size of your machine. Make sure it's nice and thick, but smooth with no lumps.

6 Transfer the hummus to a large plastic container, spread it level, then press on a well-fitting lid. Chill until needed.

500g/1lb 2oz dried chickpeas
1.2 litres/2 pints cold water
2 tsp bicarbonate of soda
300g/10½oz tahini
juice of 2 lemons
sea salt, to taste

NOTE

THE COOKING TIME MAY VARY; OLD CHICKPEAS WILL TAKE LONGER TO COOK THAN THIS SEASON'S CROP. YOU'RE AIMING FOR VERY VERY SOFT CHICKPEAS, IT DOESN'T MATTER IF THEY BREAK UP AS THEY'RE GOING TO BE BLITZED ANYWAY. IF IN DOUBT, SIMPLY SCOOP OUT A FEW CHICKPEAS, THROW THEM AT THE WALL AND IF THEY STICK, THEY'RE READY!

HOW TO ACHIEVE THE PERFECT HUMMUS BROS. SWIRL

1 Plop a large splodge of hummus onto your chosen plate – a shallow bowl is the ideal thing.

2 Take a large spoon with a rounded base – a tablespoon or large soup spoon will do the job nicely.

3 Place the spoon, bowl-side down, in the centre of the splodge and rock it back and forth until you have created a bowl-shaped cavity.

4 Pressing firmly, continue to enlarge the bowl – pressing the hummus out to the sides of your plate.

5 As you go round, push the spoon slightly under the rim of hummus – it takes practice, but you want perfection, right? This is also a test of your hummus' consistency. If you made it too watery, the crater you just created will collapse into the centre of the bowl.

6 Then, turn the spoon over onto its edge and carefully scrape it around the edge of the hummus until the sides are nice and smooth.

7 Now you're ready to fill it up with whatever takes your fancy and serve. Your friends will think your presentation skills are outstanding and you can rightfully bask in the glow of adulation!

TOPPINGS FOR HUMMUS

SERVES 4
PREP: 5 MINUTES
COOK:
40–60 MINUTES

HUMMUS WITH SLOW-COOKED CHICKPEAS

250g/9oz dried chickpeas, soaked overnight in plenty of cold water

700ml/1¼ pints cold water

1 tbsp olive oil

1 tbsp ground cumin

To finish:

450g/1lb Hummus (see p..19)

3 tbsp olive oil

juice of 1 lemon

tahini sauce

sea salt

paprika, to taste

chopped fresh flat-leaf parsley, for sprinkling

THIS IS A DOUBLE WHAMMY OF CHICKPEAS, FULL OF TASTE, NOT TO MENTION FIBRE, PROTEIN AND HEALTHY SLOW-RELEASE CARBS TO POWER YOU THROUGH THE AFTERNOON.

1 Drain the soaked chickpeas, put into a medium saucepan and pour in the water so that the chickpeas are covered by about 2cm/¾in. Add the oil and cumin and bring to the boil. Skim off any scum, if liked, then partially cover with a lid and cook over a medium heat for 40–60 minutes until the chickpeas are tender but still a good shape. Drain in a sieve set over a bowl to catch the cooking liquid.

2 Spread the Hummus over 4 serving plates and make a small well in the middle. Add a few spoonfuls of chickpeas to each well. Dress each portion with lots of olive oil, lemon juice and tahini sauce, then season to taste. Moisten with some of the reserved cooking liquid, if necessary and top with a little paprika and chopped parsley.

TIP

QUARTER A WHITE ONION AND SOAK IN A BOWL OF WATER FOR 30 MINUTES. DRAIN AND PEEL OFF THE INDIVIDUAL LAYERS, THEN USE TO SCOOP UP THE HUMMUS AND CHICKPEAS.

SERVES 4
PREP: 10 MINUTES
COOK:
17–18 MINUTES

2 tbsp olive oil

1 onion, finely diced

1 leek, thinly sliced, keeping white and green slices separated

3 spring onions, thinly sliced

2–3 garlic cloves, finely chopped

1 x 400g/14oz can chopped tomatoes

small handful of each: fresh basil, parsley and oregano, roughly chopped, plus extra to garnish

2–3 fresh thyme sprigs, leaves only

sea salt and freshly ground black pepper

400g/14oz button mushrooms, wiped and left whole

To serve:

450g/1lb Hummus (see p.19)

paprika, to taste

tahini (optional)

1 small onion, quartered, soaked and layers separated (see p.26)

HUMMUS WITH MUSHROOMS

A RICH GARLICKY, TOMATO SAUCE SPECKLED WITH THREE DIFFERENT HERBS COVERS THESE MOREISH MUSHROOMS. BASIL, PARSLEY AND OREGANO WORK VERY WELL TOGETHER, BUT DO MIX AND MATCH THE HERBS DEPENDING ON WHAT YOU HAVE IN THE FRIDGE OR GROWING IN A POT ON THE WINDOWSILL. FRESH OREGANO CAN BE DIFFICULT TO FIND, SO USE 1 TSP DRIED IF YOU CAN'T GET HOLD OF ANY.

1 Heat the oil in a large frying pan, add the onion and white sliced leeks and fry gently for 5 minutes, stirring from time to time until softened and just beginning to turn golden around the edges.

2 Add the green sliced leeks, spring onions and garlic and fry for 1–2 minutes. Mix in the tomatoes, chopped herbs and thyme leaves. Season well with salt and pepper and then bring to the boil.

3 Add the mushrooms, lower the heat, cover with a lid and simmer gently for 10 minutes, stirring from time to time until the mushrooms are just cooked. It will become more watery as the mushrooms cook and release their juices.

4 Spoon on to serving plates spread with Hummus, garnish with a few extra chopped herbs and serve with a spoonful of yogurt on the side sprinkled with a little paprika, with tahini (if using) and pieces of onion to scoop up the mushroom mix.

SERVES 4
PREP: 15 MINUTES
COOK: 1 HOUR
25 MINUTES

2 tbsp olive oil

600g/1lb 5oz skinless, boneless chicken thigh meat, cubed

1 onion, roughly chopped

2 garlic cloves, finely chopped

2 tsp sweet mild paprika

2 tsp ground cumin

1 tsp ground coriander

1 x 400g/14oz can chopped tomatoes

sea salt and freshly ground black pepper

small handful of fresh flat-leaf parsley, roughly chopped

450g/1lb Hummus (see p.19), to serve

HUMMUS WITH CHICKEN

THIS IS SO EASY TO MAKE FOR A FAMILY SUPPER OR FOR FRIENDS TO SHARE. SUCCULENT CHICKEN, LIGHTLY FRIED IN OLIVE OIL WITH GARLIC, PAPRIKA AND OUR FAVOURITE SPICES, CUMIN AND CORIANDER, THEN TOPPED WITH FRESH TASTING PARSLEY – YUM. CHEAT AND USE READY BONED AND SKINNED CHICKEN THIGHS OR BREASTS, IF YOU LIKE.

1 Heat 1 tablespoon of the oil in a large frying pan, add a few pieces of chicken at a time to the hot oil then gradually add the rest until it's all in the pan and fry over a medium heat for about 5 minutes, stirring from time to time, until golden brown, then scoop the chicken out of the pan with a slotted spoon and transfer to a plate.

2 Add the remaining oil to the frying pan, then fry the onion for 5 minutes until softened and just beginning to turn golden brown. Stir in the garlic, paprika, cumin and ground coriander and cook for 1 minute, then return the chicken to the pan and coat in the spices.

3 Pour in the tomatoes and season well with salt and pepper. Bring to the boil, then lower the heat to the lowest possible point and simmer for 1¼ hours, or until the chicken is cooked through with no hint of pink juices (a heat diffuser can help here).

4 When ready to serve, stir most of the chopped parsley into the chicken, then spoon on to serving plates spread with Hummus and sprinkle with the rest of the parsley.

HUMMUS WITH CHUNKY BEEF

2 tbsp olive oil

650g/1lb 7oz lean diced stewing beef, such as chuck steak

1 onion, chopped

1 tsp ground coriander

1 tsp ground cumin

2 tsp sweet mild paprika

1 x 400g/14oz can chopped tomatoes

300ml/½ pint beef stock

small handful of fresh coriander, roughly chopped, plus extra to garnish

small handful of fresh parsley, roughly chopped, plus extra to garnish

1 tsp coarsely ground black pepper

large pinch of sea salt

450g/1lb Hummus (see p.19), to serve

natural yogurt or Tzatziki (see p.102), to serve

GIVE AN EVERYDAY BEEF CASSEROLE A LEVANTINE-STYLE TWIST WITH OUR FAVOURITE GROUND SPICES, CUMIN AND CORIANDER, PLUS SOME CHOPPED FRESH PARSLEY, TOO. THIS WILL KEEP WELL IN THE FRIDGE FOR UP TO 3 DAYS.

1 Heat 1 tablespoon of the oil in a large frying pan, add the beef, a few pieces at a time, until all the pieces are in the pan and fry over a medium heat for about 5 minutes, stirring from time to time until browned.
Scoop out of the pan with a slotted spoon and set aside.

2 Add the remaining oil to the frying pan, then fry the onion over a medium heat for 5 minutes until softened and just beginning to turn golden brown. Stir in the ground spices and cook briefly to release their flavour, then stir in the tomatoes, stock, chopped herbs, pepper and salt. Bring to the boil, then add the beef back to the pan.

3 Turn the heat as low as it will go (a heat diffuser can help here) and cook for 2½–3 hours, or until the beef is very tender, stirring occasionally. Serve spooned on to serving plates spread with Hummus and garnished with extra chopped herbs and a spoonful of yogurt or Tzatziki on the side.

SERVES 4
PREP: 15 MINUTES
COOK:
2 HOURS 40 MINUTES–
3 HOURS 10 MINUTES

36

SERVES 4
PREP: 10 MINUTES
COOK: 45 MINUTES

HUMMUS WITH LAMB & PINE NUTS

1 tbsp olive oil

1 large red onion, finely chopped

500g/1lb 2oz minced lamb

25g/1oz butter

450ml/16fl oz lamb stock

85g/3oz bulghur wheat

2 tsp ground cumin

1½ tsp ground cinnamon

½ tsp chilli powder

1 tsp granulated sugar

sea salt and freshly ground black pepper

55g/2oz pine nuts, toasted

450g/1lb Hummus (see p.19)

To garnish:

tahini

paprika, to taste

THIS IS THE CLASSIC LEBANESE WAY OF SERVING MEAT WITH HUMMUS. THE CINAMMON–FLAVOURED MEAT AND NUTS BLEND PERFECTLY WITH THE HUMMUS. SERVED HERE WITH A LITTLE GREEN CHILLI SAUCE (SEE P.104) ON THE SIDE.

1 Heat the oil in a large frying pan, add the onion and fry over a medium heat for 5 minutes, stirring until just beginning to brown around the edges. Add the lamb and butter and fry, stirring from time to time and breaking up the mince with a wooden spoon until browned and tender.

2 Meanwhile, bring the stock to the boil in a saucepan, add the bulghur wheat, cover, lower the heat and simmer for 10 minutes until just tender with just enough stock left to keep the bulghur wheat moist.

3 Add the cumin, cinnamon and chilli powder to the mince, then stir in the sugar and season with salt and pepper. Cover with a lid and cook for 10 minutes. Tip the bulghur wheat and stock into the mince, then about two-thirds of the pine nuts. Stir together, cover and cook gently for 10 minutes.

4 Spoon on to serving plates spread with Hummus, then sprinkle with the rest of the pine nuts. Add a spoonful of tahini, sprinkle with a little paprika to garnish and serve.

HUMMUS WITH LAMB ROGAN JOSH

2 tbsp olive oil

1 onion, very finely chopped (blitz in a food processor if you have one)

650g/1lb 7oz bonelss shoulder of lamb, cut into large dice

2.5cm/1in piece fresh root ginger, grated

2 garlic cloves, finely chopped

½ tsp chilli powder

1 tsp turmeric

1 tsp garam masala

1 tsp ground coriander

2 tsp ground cumin

¼ tsp sea salt

200g/7oz tomatoes, diced

150ml/¼ pint water

100g/3½oz Greek yogurt

450g/1lb Hummus (see p.19), to serve

chopped fresh coriander, to garnish

IT MIGHT SEEM A STRANGE COMBO – INDIAN CURRY WITH HUMMUS, BUT OUR CUSTOMERS JUST LOVE IT. ALWAYS BUY DICED SHOULDER OF LAMB IF YOU CAN, AS THE MEAT HAS A NATURAL SWEETNESS AND JUST MELTS IN THE MOUTH COOKED THIS WAY, BUT A SUPERMARKET PACK OF READY-DICED LAMB WORKS WELL, TOO.

1 Heat the oil in a large frying pan, add the onion and fry over a low heat for 3–4 minutes, stirring until softened. Add the lamb, a few pieces at a time, until all the pieces are in the pan. Fry over a medium heat for 10 minutes, stirring from time to time until the lamb is browned.

2 Stir in the ginger and garlic, then mix in the ground spices and salt. Cover with a lid and cook for 20–25 minutes, stirring from time to time, until the spices form a crust around the lamb and the oil has begun to separate slightly.

3 Add the tomatoes and water, re-cover and cook for 30 minutes, stirring from time to time, until the lamb is meltingly tender. Take off the heat and stir in the yogurt.

4 Spoon on to serving plates spread with Hummus and sprinkle with a little chopped coriander before serving.

SERVES 4
PREP: 20 MINUTES
COOK: 1 HOUR –
1 HOUR 10 MINUTES

HUMMUS WITH CHILLI CON CARNE

SERVES 4
PREP: 15 MINUTES
COOK: 1 HOUR
10 MINUTES

1 tbsp olive oil

1 onion, finely chopped

500g/1lb 2oz fresh lean beef mince

½ each of red, green and yellow peppers, cored, deseeded and diced

2 garlic cloves, finely chopped

1 carrot, diced

½ tsp ground cinnamon

1 tsp ground cumin

1 tsp chilli powder

1 tsp coarsely crushed ground black pepper

sea salt

1 x 400g/14oz can chopped tomatoes

1 tbsp granulated sugar

1 x 400g/14oz can red kidney beans, drained

up to 300ml/½ pint beef stock

To serve:

450g/1lb Hummus (see p.19)

sour cream

Guacamole (see p.100)

SERVING THIS FAVOURITE ON A BED OF HUMMUS WILL GET YOUR FRIENDS TALKING, BUT THE CREAMY SMOOTHNESS OF THE HUMMUS REALLY WORKS WELL WITH THE MELLOW HEAT OF THE CHILLI AND MAKES A CHANGE FROM PLAIN BOILED RICE. IT'S DELICIOUS TOPPED WITH SOUR CREAM AND GUACAMOLE, OR, IF YOU LIKE YOUR FOOD EXTRA HOT, TRY THIS TOPPED WITH A SPOONFUL OF GREEN CHILLI SAUCE (SEE P.104).

1 Heat the oil in a large saucepan, add the onion and fry over a medium heat for 5 minutes, stirring from time to time until softened and just beginning to turn golden. Stir in the beef and fry for 20 minutes, stirring and breaking up the mince with a wooden spoon until browned and tender.

2 Stir in the diced peppers, garlic and carrot and cook for a few minutes to soften. Stir in the ground spices, pepper and sea salt and cook for a further 1–2 minutes to bring out all the flavours.

3 Mix in the tomatoes, sugar, drained kidney beans and stock. Bring to the boil, then cover with a lid, lower the heat to very low and cook for 40 minutes, stirring from time to time.

4 Spoon on to serving plates spread with Hummus, then top with spoonfuls of sour cream and Guacamole.

40

SERVES 4
PREP: 10 MINUTES
COOK:
45 MINUTES

HUMMUS WITH MEXICAN BEEF

1 tbsp olive oil
1 onion, chopped
500g/1lb 2oz fresh beef mince
2 garlic cloves, finely chopped
2 tsp sweet mild paprika
1 tsp ground cumin
1 tsp ground coriander
½ tsp chilli powder
1 tsp granulated sugar
sea salt and freshly ground
black pepper
300ml/½ pint beef stock
1 tbsp tomato purée

To serve:
450g/1lb Hummus (see p.19)
grated cheese
Tomato & Coriander Salsa (see p.103)
or Guacamole (see p.100)
crushed tortilla chips
warm Pitta Breads (see p.110)
Green Chilli Sauce (see p.104),
optional

THIS RECIPE IS THE BRAINCHILD OF OUR ORIGINAL MARKETING MANAGER, AN AMERICAN FROM FLORIDA, WHO JUST KNEW THIS COMBINATION WOULD WORK WELL. WE RECENTLY CONDUCTED A SURVEY OF FAVOURITE TOPPINGS AND MEXICAN BEEF CAME OUT ON TOP. THANK YOU RYAN!

1 Heat the oil in a large frying pan, add the onion and fry over a medium heat for 5 minutes, stirring until just beginning to brown around the edges. Add the beef and fry for 20 minutes, stirring and breaking up the mince with a wooden spoon until browned and tender.

2 Add the garlic, ground spices and chilli powder to the mince, then stir in the sugar and season with salt and pepper. Cover with a lid and cook for 10 minutes, then mix in the stock and tomato purée. Re-cover and cook for 10 minutes.

3 Spoon on to serving plates spread with Hummus, then top with grated cheese and spoonfuls of Tomato & Coriander Salsa or Guacamole. Sprinkle crushed tortilla chips on top. Serve with warm Pitta Breads and Green Chilli Sauce, if liked.

HUMMUS WITH MOROCCAN MEATBALLS

125g/4½oz sliced bread, torn into pieces

500g/1lb 2oz fresh extra lean beef mince

2 eggs

1 tsp chilli powder

½ tsp ground cinnamon

sea salt and freshly ground black pepper

450g/1lb Hummus (see p.19), to serve

fresh parsley or basil leaves, to garnish

For the tomato sauce:

1 tbsp olive oil

1 onion, finely chopped

2 celery sticks, finely chopped

2–3 garlic cloves, finely chopped

½ tsp chilli powder

2 x 400g/14oz cans chopped tomatoes

2 tsp granulated sugar

SERVES 4
PREP: 20 MINUTES
COOK: 30 MINUTES

CHRISTIAN: THIS IS MY FAVOURITE TOPPING BY FAR AND IT GOES PARTICULARLY WELL WITH GUACAMOLE. MEATBALLS ARE ALWAYS POPULAR IN THE RESTAURANT, BUT PEOPLE ARE PUT OFF MAKING THEM AT HOME AS THEY THINK THEY'RE FIDDLY. IF YOU HAVE A FOOD PROCESSOR THEN JUST BUNG EVERYTHING IN TOGETHER AND BLITZ IN SECONDS. THEN JUST ADD THE MEATBALLS TO OUR EASY TOMATO SAUCE AND LET THEM SIMMER GENTLY WHILE YOU GET ON WITH SOMETHING ELSE.

1 Blitz the bread in a food processor until fine crumbs form. Add the beef mince and eggs, then spoon in the chilli powder and cinnamon. Season generously with salt and pepper, then blitz together until well mixed. If you don't have a food processor, make breadcrumbs in a blender or rub over a coarse grater, then mix with the remaining ingredients in a bowl.

2 Using a dessertspoon, scoop out the meatball mixture on to a chopping board or baking sheet to make 24 mounds, then shape into balls by hand.

3 For the sauce, heat the oil in a large, deep frying pan with a lid, add the onion and celery and fry for 5 minutes over a low heat until soft and just beginning to turn golden. Stir in the garlic and chilli powder, then the tomatoes and sugar. Season with salt and pepper, then cover and simmer gently for 5 minutes.

4 Take the lid off the pan and add the meatballs, in a single layer if there's room. Cover and cook over a low heat for 15 minutes. Uncover, turn the meatballs and cook for a further 5 minutes until the sauce has thickened and the meatballs are cooked through. To test if they are cooked, take out one of the meatballs and cut it in half – there should be no hint of pink.

5 Spoon on to serving plates spread with Hummus and top with parsley or basil or a mixture of them both.

MASABACHA

1 quantity of hot Slow-cooked Chickpeas (see p.26), with a little of their cooking liquid

450g/1lb Hummus (see p.19)
225g/8oz plain tahini

To serve:
4-6 tbsp olive oil
1-2 lemons, juiced or cut into wedges
4 x hard-boiled eggs, peeled and quartered
1 tsp ground cumin
1 tsp sweet mild paprika
large handful of fresh flat-leaf parsley, roughly torn
2-3 garlic cloves, finely chopped (optional)
warm Pitta Breads (see p.110) or onion scoops (see p.26)

NOT FOR THE FAINT HEARTED! MASABACHA IS FOR HUMMUS FANATICS WHO WANT TO TAKE IT TO THE NEXT LEVEL – IT HAS INDULGENCE WRITTEN ALL OVER IT. A MAIN MEAL IN ISRAELI CULTURE, COMMONLY SERVED WARM, IT HAS A UNIQUE COMBINATION OF TEXTURES (CHEWY CHICKPEAS, SMOOTH HUMMUS, STICKY TAHINI). IT'S A HEAVENLY MIXTURE.

WHATEVER YOU ADD HERE, MAKE SURE THERE'S LOTS OF IT: HUMMUS, TAHINI, LEMON AND COPIOUS QUANTITIES OF OLIVE OIL. SLICE AN EGG ON TOP (HARD-BOILED FOR 8 HOURS IF YOU'RE A PURIST, ALTHOUGH A 10-MINUTE EGG IS FINE TOO) AND SPRINKLE WITH ROUGHLY CHOPPED PARSLEY AND GARLIC (ONLY IF YOU'RE INTO GARLIC – IT'S NOT ESSENTIAL). NOW DIVE IN WITH FRESH PITTA OR A SCOOP OF ONION. AND DON'T EXPECT TO GET MUCH WORK DONE AFTER THE FEAST!

1 In a large pan, warm the Chickpeas with a bit of their liquid, then throw in a dollop of Hummus, then the tahini and gently mix together to warm through. Sprinkle with plenty of olive oil and lemon juice. Don't leave in the pan very long – just 30 seconds to get the Hummus mixing with the chickpeas and warming up. The whole thing should be served at just above room temperature, not hot.

2 Divide the mixture between deep bowls and add the quartered egg. Season to taste with extra lemon juice, olive oil, cumin and paprika, then top with plenty of parsley. Serve with fresh lemon juice (with finely chopped garlic on the side, if you like), or for a more visual effect, add a lemon wedge rather than the juice mixture – it adds colour. Serve with warm Pitta Breads or onion scopps.

NOTES

Always make sure the dish is swimming in plenty of lemon and oil, but do put the garlic on the side as an option and let your guests decide if they want it.

Pitta bread has a tendency to dry out if not kept properly covered. If you have pitta breads that are not 100 per cent fresh, sprinkle a tiny amount of water over and put in a warm oven for 2-3 minutes (watch carefully) to revive them.

SERVES 4
PREP: 15 MINUTES
COOK: 8 MINUTES

SERVES 4
PREP: 15 MINUTES
COOK: 45–60

HUMMUS WITH FAVA BEANS

250g/9oz dried split fouls medames, or fava beans, soaked overnight in cold water

700ml/1¼ pints cold water

2 tbsp olive oil

juice of 1 lemon

2 tsp ground cumin

sea salt and freshly ground black pepper

To finish:

450g/1lb Hummus (see p.19)

extra virgin olive oil

small handful of fresh parsley, finely chopped

ground cumin

chilli sauce

lemon wedges

warm Pitta Breads (see p.110) or 2 onions, quartered, soaked and layers separated (see p.26)

4 x hardboiled eggs (optional)

THE TRADITIONAL WAY OF EATING BREAKFAST HUMMUS, ORIGINATING IN EGYPTIAN CUISINE. MANUAL WORKERS WOULD HAVE THIS FOR BREAKFAST IN ANTICIPATION OF A HARD WORKING DAY AHEAD. FAVA BEANS ARE NOT ALWAYS EASY TO FIND, BUT DO MAKE THE EFFORT AS THEY'RE VERY HEALTHY AND THE WHOLE DISH IS JUST SO DISTINCTIVE – NOTHING ELSE TASTES QUITE LIKE IT. SLICE AN EGG ON TOP TO MAKE IT EVEN MORE AUTHENTIC IF YOU WISH. DRIZZLE WITH PLENTY OF OLIVE OIL, LEMON JUICE, PARSLEY AND A BIT OF CUMIN, AND LET THE FLAVOURS TRANSPORT YOU TO A FAR AWAY LAND.

1 Drain the soaked beans, put into a medium saucepan and pour in the water so that the beans are covered by about 2cm/¾in. Add olive oil, lemon juice, cumin and plenty of salt and black pepper, then bring to the boil. Partially cover with a lid and cook over a medium heat for about 45–60 minutes, or until the beans are very soft and mash easily between 2 fingers.

2 Pour the beans into a colander set above a bowl to catch the cooking liquid, then tip half the beans back into the empty pan with a little of the reserved cooking liquid. Grind with a stick blender, or transfer the beans and liquid to a food processor and blitz, gradually adding more of the cooking liquid as needed to make a thick spreadable consistency. If you have been a bit heavy handed with the liquid then add a few more beans. Once you get the texture right, gradually add more beans and a little more cooking liquid until all the beans have been ground. Taste and adjust the seasoning as needed.

3 Spread the Hummus over serving plates, then top with spoonfuls of the warm fava bean mix. Finish with plenty of extra olive oil and chopped parsley and serve with chilli sauce and lemon wedges to squeeze over, and warmed Pitta Breads or pieces of onion to scoop up the bean mix. Slices of hardboiled egg will complete the dish, but you can leave them off if you prefer.

SHAKSHUKA

750g/1lb 10oz plum tomatoes

2 tbsp olive oil

2 onions, finely chopped

1–1½ large mild red chillies, deseeded and finely chopped

100g/3½oz chorizo sausage, thinly sliced

1 tbsp tomato purée

1½ tsp caster sugar

1 tsp smoked mild paprika

sea salt and freshly ground black pepper

4–8 eggs

1 tsp dried oregano

crusty bread or cholla, to serve

IDEAL FOR SATURDAY BRUNCH, THIS IS ONE OF THOSE RECIPES THAT THE MORE YOU MAKE IT THE BETTER IT WILL BE; ONLY BY MAKING IT 20 TIMES WILL YOU GET PERFECT RESULTS! SERVE ONE OR TWO EGGS PER PORTION DEPENDING ON HOW HUNGRY YOUR BRUNCH GUESTS ARE. YOU MIGHT LIKE TO EXPERIMENT WITH EXTRA INGREDIENTS: MORE CHILLI OR MORE CHORIZO, SPRING ONIONS TO GARNISH, EVEN DICED MOZZARELLA SPRINKLED OVER AT THE VERY END.

1 Make a cross cut in the base of each tomato, put into a heatproof bowl and pour over boiling water to just cover them. Leave to stand for 1 minute until the skins begin to peel away, then drain and rinse with cold water until cool enough to handle. Peel away the skins with a sharp knife. Chop the tomatoes into 1cm/½in dice, leaving in the seeds.

2 Heat the oil in a large frying pan, add the onions and chillies and fry for 2–3 minutes until just beginning to soften. Add the chorizo and cook for a further 2–3 minutes until the onion is beginning to colour with the chorizo juices.

SERVES 4
PREP: 15 MINUTES
COOK: 1 HOUR

3 Stir in the tomatoes, tomato purée and sugar, then add the paprika and salt and pepper. Cover and cook over a low heat for 30 minutes, stirring every 10 minutes or so until the

tomatoes are really soft. Keep a watchful eye as they cook – if the heat is a little high you may need to stir in a little extra water to stop them drying out completely.

4 When the mixture is quite dry (but not burnt), uncover and stir the sauce, then with a large spoon make little dips or craters large enough to hold the eggs. Try not to position the dips too close to the edge of the pan. If the sauce is a little too runny then simmer over a slightly higher heat, stirring for 5 minutes or so until it has thickened. Carefully break an egg into each dip, being careful not to break the yolks. Sprinkle the oregano and a little extra salt over the yolks, then re-cover the pan and cook gently for 5–10 minutes until the egg whites are set and the yolks cooked to your liking. You are aiming to poach/steam the eggs rather than fry them. Serve with some crusty bread or cholla.

50

SERVES 4
PREP: 15 MINUTES
COOK:
22–28 MINUTES

HUMMUS WITH SPICY SAUSAGE & 3 PEPPER STEW

2 tbsp olive oil

1 onion, chopped

1 red pepper, halved, cored, deseeded and diced

1 green pepper, halved, cored, deseeded and diced

1 yellow pepper, halved, cored, deseeded and diced

300g/10oz Kabanos Polish sausage, thickly sliced

500g/1lb 2oz plum tomatoes (no need to peel), diced

2 courgettes, diced

2 red chillies, halved, deseeded and finely chopped

sea salt and freshly ground black pepper

1 tbsp tomato purée

1–2 green chillies, halved, deseeded and finely chopped

450g/1lb Hummus (see p.19), to serve

PACKED WITH COLOURFUL MEDITERRANEAN VEGETABLES, THIS STOVE-TOP STEW IS FLAVOURED WITH RED AND GREEN CHILLIES. THE AMOUNT YOU USE IS VERY MUCH UP TO YOU. IF YOU LIKE YOUR FOOD HOT AND SPICY THEN ADJUST THE HEAT AT THE END WHEN ADDING THE GREEN CHILLI.

1 Heat the oil in a large, deep frying pan with a lid, add the onion and diced peppers and fry over a medium heat for 10–15 minutes, stirring from time to time, until the peppers are softened.

2 Stir in the sliced Polish sausage, the tomatoes, courgettes and red chillies. Season generously with salt and pepper, then cover and cook for 10 minutes, stirring from time to time, until the tomatoes are softened and saucy.

3 Mix in the tomato purée, then gradually add half the green chillies and cook for 2–3 minutes. Taste and adjust with extra chilli to taste.

4 Spoon on to serving plates spread with Hummus, then drizzle with the pan juices and serve piping hot.

SERVES 4
PREP: 30 MINUTES
MARINATE: 6 HOURS,
OR OVERNIGHT
COOK: 46 MINUTES–
1 HOUR

HUMMUS WITH CHICKEN TIKKA MASALA

200g/7oz Greek yogurt
2 tsp ground coriander
2 tsp sweet mild paprika
1 tsp garam masala
1 tsp ground ginger
½ tsp ground cinnamon
¼ tsp chilli powder
4 cardamom pods, crushed, black seeds ground in a pestle and mortar, green pods discarded
2 garlic cloves, finely chopped
2 tbsp white wine vinegar or fresh lemon juice
1 tbsp tomato purée
½ tsp sea salt
55g/2oz broken cashew nuts, plus a few extra to garnish
650g/1lb 7oz skinless, boneless chicken breast, cubed
55g/2oz unsalted butter
1 onion, very finely chopped (blitz in a food processor if you have one)
150ml/¼ pint double cream
fresh coriander leaves, torn, to garnish
450g/1lb Hummus (see p.19), to serve

FED UP WITH RICE? THEN TRY OUR TAKE ON THIS FAVOURITE INDIAN CURRY. DON'T BE PUT OFF BY THE LONG LIST OF SPICES; CHANCES ARE YOU WILL HAVE MOST OF THEM ALREADY.

1 The day before serving or at least 7 hours in advance, put the yogurt into a large glass or china shallow bowl. Add all the spices, garlic, vinegar or lemon juice, tomato purée and salt and mix together with a spoon.

2 Preheat the oven to 150°C/300°F/Gas mark 2 or heat the grill to medium.

3 Toast the cashew nut pieces, including a few extra ones for the garnish, either in the oven for 10 minutes, stirring from time to time until golden, or under the grill for 4–5 minutes. Leave to cool, then blitz in a blender or food processor and stir into the yogurt marinade with the chicken, mixing well so that the chicken is evenly coated. Cover the dish with clingfilm and chill in the fridge for 6 hours, or overnight.

4 The next day, heat the butter in a frying pan, add the onion and fry gently for 3–4 minutes, stirring until just beginning to colour. Add the chicken and yogurt marinade to the pan and cook for 30–40 minutes, stirring from time to time until the chicken is tender and cooked through. To check, lift one of the chicken pieces out of the pan, cut in half and check there is no sign of pink juices.

5 Stir in the cream and warm through gently for 3 minutes. Spoon on to serving plates spread with Hummus and garnish with extra toasted cashew nuts and torn coriander.

FINGERS WERE MADE BEFORE FORKS

FALAFEL AND WRAPS

SERVES 4–6
PREP: 20 MINUTES
CHILL: 30 MINUTES
COOK: 15 MINUTES

GREEN FALAFEL

250g/9oz dried chickpeas, soaked overnight in plenty of cold water

1 white onion, roughly chopped

small handful of fresh flat-leaf parsley

small handful of fresh mint sprigs, leaves torn from stems

small handful of fresh coriander

2 garlic cloves, sliced

1 tsp ground cumin

1 tsp ground coriander

1 tsp bicarbonate of soda

2 tsp black onion seeds

salt and freshly ground black pepper

3 tbsp sesame seeds

1 litre/1¾ pints sunflower oil, for deep-frying

To serve:

Pitta Breads (see p.110)

Hummus (see p.19)

shredded lettuce

sliced tomatoes

tahini sauce or tzatziki and chilli sauce

FALAFEL IS THE MIDDLE EASTERN VERSION OF FAST FOOD. THE BALLS CAN BE SERVED ON THEIR OWN, IN PITTA OR A MEZZE, OR WITH A BOWL OF HUMMUS. WE OFTEN SERVE THEM ON A BED OF SHREDDED CABBAGE AND LETTUCE, WITH A TOMATO & CORIANDER SALSA (P.103), TZATZIKI (P.102) AND OLIVE OIL.

A HAND MINCER IS THE BEST PIECE OF EQUIPMENT FOR MAKING FALAFEL, AS PEOPLE TEND TO OVER-BLITZ THE MIXTURE IN A FOOD PROCESSOR. FOR THE BEST TEXTURE, DO USE A MINCER IF YOU HAVE ONE.

1 Drain the soaked chickpeas well in a colander.

2 If using a mincer, put all the ingredients, except the spices and seeds, through the mincer, and then mix together.

3 If using a food processor, blitz the onion, herbs and garlic until finely chopped. Add the spices, bicarb, onion seeds, 1 teaspoon of salt and pepper to taste. Scoop into a bowl and set aside. Blitz the chickpeas only very gently until just broken up, in two batches if necessary, then mix into the herb mixture.

4 Cover and chill in the fridge for about 30 minutes.

5 Shape into 16–20 portions, then press firmly into balls with damp hands. Roll in the sesame seeds before frying.

6 Heat the oil for deep-frying in a pan to 180°C/350°F (a square of day-old bread should immediately sizzle in it). Lower 4 falafels into the oil and cook for 3–4 minutes until golden on the outside but so that you can still see the green of the herbs. Remove with a slotted spoon to a plate lined with kitchen paper. Test that they are done by cutting one in half; they should be cooked through and light and fluffy on the inside.

7 Check the temperature of the oil and continue frying the remaining falafel in batches until they are all cooked. Serve tucked into Pitta Breads, with Hummus, lettuce, tomatoes and tahini sauce or tzatziki/chilli sauce.

NOTE

BEST MADE WITH DRIED SOAKED CHICKPEAS THAT ARE GROUND BEFORE COOKING FOR A LIGHTER TEXTURED FALAFEL. CANNED CHICKPEAS MAKE A WETTER MIXTURE WITH A DENSER TEXTURE.

58

SERVES 4–6
PREP: 30 MINUTES
CHILL: 30 MINUTES
COOK: 25–30 MINUTES

SWEET POTATO FALAFEL

250g/9oz sweet potato, peeled and diced

250g/9oz dried chickpeas, soaked overnight in cold water

1 onion, roughly chopped

2 garlic cloves, sliced

2.5cm/1in piece fresh root ginger, peeled and finely chopped

1 tsp ground turmeric

1 tsp ground coriander

1 tsp bicarbonate of soda

salt and freshly ground black pepper

1 litre/1¾ pints sunflower oil, for deep-frying

To serve (optional):

450g/1lb Hummus (see p.19)

300g/10½oz Tahini Sauce (see p.98)

Mixed Vegetable Salad (see p.88)

TRADITIONALISTS MAY THROW THEIR HANDS UP IN HORROR BUT WE LIKE TO EXPERIMENT WITH DIFFERENT FLAVOURED FALAFEL. WE HOPE YOU LIKE THIS DELICIOUS SWEET POTATO, GINGER AND TURMERIC VERSION.

1 Pour water into the base of a steamer, bring to the boil, and add the sweet potato to the top of the steamer. Cover and cook for 10–15 minutes, depending on the size of the potato chunks, until tender when pressed with a knife.

2 Drain the chickpeas in a colander. Put the onion, garlic and ginger into a food processor and finely chop. Add the ground spices, bicarb, 1 teaspoon of salt and pepper to taste and blitz together briefly. Scoop out into a bowl.

3 Put chickpeas through a mincer, or add small batches of them to the food processor and briefly blitz until just broken up, scraping down the sides of the bowl every now and again. Transfer to the bowl, adding the sweet potato with the last batch of chickpeas.

4 Stir the falafel mix together, then cover and chill in the fridge for about 30 minutes.

5 Shape into 24 portions, then press firmly into balls with damp hands.

6 Heat the oil for deep-frying in a pan to 180°C/350°F (a square of day-old bread should immediately sizzle in it). Carefully lower 4 falafel into the oil and cook for 3–4 minutes until deep golden on the outside and light and fluffy on the inside. Remove with a slotted spoon to a plate lined with kitchen paper. Check the temperature of the oil and continue frying the falafel in batches until they are all cooked.

7 Serve on plates swirled with Hummus, drizzled with Tahini Sauce and accompanied by some Mixed Vegetable Salad.

COOK'S TIP

IF YOU ARE MAKING UP LARGE BATCHES OF FALAFEL, YOU MIGHT LIKE TO SHAPE THEM WITH A SMALL DAMP ICE CREAM SCOOP AND FLATTEN THEM SLIGHTLY INTO PATTY SHAPES, AS THESE COOK MUCH QUICKER IN QUANTITY THAN BALLS.

SPICY RED FALAFEL

250g/9oz trimmed beetroot, peeled and diced

250g/9oz dried chickpeas, soaked overnight in plenty of cold water

1 red onion, roughly chopped

2 garlic cloves, sliced

small handful of fresh coriander, torn

1 large red chilli, deseeded and chopped

1 tsp paprika

1 tsp ground cumin

1 tsp bicarbonate of soda

salt and freshly ground black pepper

1 litre/1¾ pints sunflower oil, for deep-frying

To serve (optional):

450g/1lb Hummus (see p.19)

300g/10oz Tahini Sauce (see p.98)

1 quantity Tomato & Coriander Salsa (see p.103)

SERVES 4–6
PREP: 30 MINUTES
CHILL: 30 MINUTES
COOK: 35 MINUTES

BEETROOT ADDS THE MOST AMAZING COLOUR TO THESE HOT CHILLI, CUMIN AND PAPRIKA FALAFEL. FOR EXTRA HEAT SERVE WITH TOMATO & CORIANDER SALSA (P.103) OR GREEN CHILLI SAUCE (P.104), OR FOR THOSE WHO LOVE THAT HOT AND COLD SENSATION, TOP WITH SPOONFULS OF CREAMY TZATZIKI (P.102) AND SALT-PICKLED CUCUMBERS (P.146).

1 Pour water into the base of a steamer, bring to the boil, and add the beetroot to the top of the steamer. Cover and cook for 20 minutes, or until tender when pressed with a knife.

2 Drain the chickpeas in a colander. Put the onion, garlic, coriander and chilli into a food processor and finely chop. Add the ground spices, bicarb, 1 teaspoon of salt and pepper to taste and blitz together briefly. Scoop out into a bowl.

3 Put chickpeas through a mincer, or add small batches of them to the food processor and briefly blitz until just broken up, scraping down the sides of the bowl every now and again. Spoon into a bowl and set aside.

4 Blitz the beetroot until finely mashed. Stir into the chickpea mix, cover and chill in the fridge for 30 minutes.

5 Shape into 24 portions, then press firmly into balls with damp hands.

6 Heat the oil for deep-frying in a pan to 180°C/350°F (a square of day-old bread should immediately sizzle in it). Carefully lower 4 falafel into the oil and cook for 3–4 minutes until deep golden on the outside and light and fluffy on the inside. Remove with a slotted spoon to a plate lined with kitchen paper. Check the temperature of the oil and continue frying the falafels in batches until they are all cooked.

7 Serve on plates swirled with Hummus, drizzled with Tahini Sauce and topped with Tomato & Coriander Salsa.

MIXED BEAN FALAFEL

85g/3oz dried fava (broad) beans, soaked overnight in plenty of cold water

85g/3oz dried chickpeas, soaked overnight in plenty of cold water

85g/3oz green lentils, soaked overnight in plenty of cold water

1 onion, chopped

2 garlic cloves, sliced

small handful of fresh coriander leaves, torn

grated rind and juice 1 lemon

1 tsp ground allspice

1 tsp paprika

1 tsp bicarbonate of soda

salt and freshly ground black pepper

1 litre/1¾ pints sunflower oil, for deep-frying

To serve (optional):

450g/1lb Hummus (see p.19)

300g/10½oz Green Tahini Sauce (see p.98)

Fatoush Salad (see p.92)

SERVES 4–6
PREP: 30 MINUTES
CHILL: 30 MINUTES
COOK: 15 MINUTES

FALAFEL DON'T HAVE TO BE MADE JUST WITH CHICKPEAS. A MIXTURE OF CHICKPEAS, FAVA BEANS AND LENTILS ALSO TASTE GREAT WHEN FLAVOURED WITH TANGY LEMON AND A LITTLE GROUND ALLSPICE.

1 Drain the fava beans, chickpeas and lentils well in a colander. Put the onion, garlic and coriander leaves into a food processor and blitz until finely chopped. Add the lemon rind, ground spices, bicarb, 1 teaspoon of salt and pepper to taste and blitz together briefly. Scoop into a bowl and set aside.

2 Put the drained (soaked) pulses through a mincer, or add small batches of them to the food processor and briefly blitz until just broken up, scraping down the sides of the bowl every now and again. Gradually mix in more of the pulses and the lemon juice until they are a coarse paste.

3 Mix the pulse mixture into the onion mixture. Cover and chill in the fridge for 30 minutes.

4 Shape into 24 portions, then press firmly into balls with damp hands..

5 Heat the oil for deep-frying in a pan to 180°C/350°F (a square of day-old bread should immediately sizzle in it). Carefully lower 4 falafel into the oil and cook for 3–4 minutes until deep golden on the outside and light and fluffy on the inside. Remove with a slotted spoon to a plate lined with kitchen paper. Check the temperature of the oil and continue frying the falafel in batches until they are all cooked.

6 Serve on plates swirled with Hummus, drizzled with the Green Tahini Sauce and accompanied by the Fatoush Salad.

FALAFEL WRAPS

oil, for deep-frying
8 shaped but not cooked Falafel
(see p.56)
2 large flat wraps
100g/3½oz Hummus (see p.19)
Salt-pickled Cucumbers (see p.146)
Tahini Sauce (see p.98)
1 large tomato, thinly sliced
cabbage or lettuce, thinly sliced
chilli sauce

SERVES 2
PREP: 15 MINUTES
COOK: 6–8 MINUTES

FALAFEL IS ONE OF THOSE DISHES THAT DOESN'T TASTE AMAZING ON ITS OWN; IT NEEDS TO BE BALANCED WITH OTHER INGREDIENTS. THAT'S WHY WRAPS OR PITTAS WORK SO WELL. THE ESSENTIAL COMPONENTS OF A FALAFEL WRAP ARE: HUMMUS (TEXTURE), TOMATO (ACIDITY), CHILLI SAUCE (SPICE), TAHINI SAUCE (LEMONY), PICKLED CUCUMBERS (SALTY) WITH SOME CABBAGE OR LETTUCE (FOR CRUNCH). OTHER OPTIONAL INGREDIENTS INCLUDE GUACAMOLE, FRIED AUBERGINE SLICES, PICKLED BEETROOT OR OTHER ROOT VEG, AND FRIES.

RONEN: MY FAVOURITE FALAFEL CAME FROM A LITTLE SHOP IN TEL AVIV CALLED "THE QUEENS OF FALAFEL". OWNED BY 2 LADIES, THEY SERVED 3 TYPES: GREEN (CORIANDER AND PARSLEY), ORANGE (SWEET POTATO) AND RED (CHILLIES). SEE THE CONNECTION?! THE PITTA BREAD WAS ALWAYS SO MOIST AND CHEWY AND THE FALAFEL BALLS MELTED INTO THE BREAD BEAUTIFULLY. UNFORTUNATELY THEY CLOSED DOWN A FEW YEARS AGO, BUT LUCKILY WE'D OPENED OUR FIRST BRANCH BY THEN SO I COULD EAT OURS EVERY DAY.

1 Heat the oil for deep-frying in a pan to 180°C/350°F (a square of day-old bread should immediately sizzle in it). Cook the Falafel in batches for 3–4 minutes until browned and crisp on the outside and light and fluffy on the inside. Remove with a slotted spoon to a plate lined with kitchen paper.

2 Warm the wraps, one at a time, in a hot dry frying pan for 1–2 minutes each. Transfer to a large board, spread with the Hummus, top with the hot Falafel, Pickled Cucumbers, tomato slices and cabbage/lettuce. Drizzle with Tahini Sauce and chilli sauce. Fold each wrap around the Falafel to make a parcel, then serve.

SABICH: AUBERGINE & EGG WRAP

2 hard-boiled eggs,
cooked for 8 hours

1 aubergine, cut into long thin slices

salt

4 tbsp sunflower oil

2 large flat wraps

100g/3½oz Hummus (see p.19)

100g/3½oz Tomato & Coriander
Salsa (see p.103)

few slices of Salt-pickled Cucumber
(see p.146), sliced lengthways

Tahini Sauce (see p.98)

To serve:

Tzatziki (see p.102)

SERVES 2
PREP: 45 MINUTES
(PLUS 8 HOURS FOR
THE EGGS,
IF WISHED)
COOK: 6–8 MINUTES

THIS IRAQI SPECIALITY IS MADE WITH EGGS THAT HAVE BEEN COOKED LONG AND SLOW. YOU CAN BOIL THEM FOR 2–3 HOURS, IF YOU LIKE, BUT IN THE RESTAURANT WE COOK THEM FOR 8 HOURS! DON'T BE ALARMED WHEN YOU PEEL AND CUT INTO THEM, AS THE EGG WHITE WILL HAVE TAKEN ON A BROWNISH COLOUR, BUT THEY WILL NOW BE RICH IN CALCIUM, WHICH HAS BEEN ABSORBED FROM THE SHELL. JUST REMEMBER TO WATCH THE PAN AND TOP UP WITH WARM WATER WHEN THE LEVEL GETS A LITTLE LOW – IT'S EASY TO FORGET ABOUT THEM AND BOIL THE PAN DRY. IF STRETCHED FOR TIME, CHEAT THE COLOUR BY THROWING A TEA BAG INTO THE WATER.

1 Peel the eggs, cut each one into 4 wedges and set aside.

2 Spread the aubegine slices out on some kitchen paper, sprikle with salt and leave to "sweat" for 30 minutes. Then rinse and pat dry.

3 Heat the oil in a large frying pan and fry the aubergine slices on both sides for 4–5 minutes until golden. Alternatively, brush the slices with a little oil and cook under a preheated grill.

4 Warm the wraps in the dried aubergine pan, then take out and put on plates. Spread each one with some of the Hummus, then top with the aubergine slices. Spoon the Tomato & Coriander Salsa on top, then add the egg and Pickled Cucumbers. Finally drizzle with plenty of Tahini Sauce.

5 Fold the wraps tightly around the fillings, turn over so that the joins are underneath on the plate, cut in half and serve with Tzatziki on the side.

BEEF WRAPS

4 large flat wraps

225g/8oz Hummus (see p..19)

4 cos lettuce leaves

100g/3½oz Tomato & Coriander Salsa (see p.19)

2 Salt-pickled Cucumbers (see p.146) or shop-bought, drained and cut into long strips

1 quantity hot beef casserole from Hummus with Chunky Beef (see p.35),

SERVES 4
PREP: 15 MINUTES
COOK:
3 MINUTES

TRANSFORM SOME LEFTOVER BEEF CASSEROLE INTO LUNCH OR ANOTHER SUPPER WITH THESE TASTY WRAPS. OR WHY NOT MAKE A DOUBLE QUANTITY OF CASSEROLE AND FREEZE IN SMALLER PORTIONS FOR ANOTHER NIGHT WHEN YOU ARE TOO TIRED TO COOK FROM SCRATCH.

1 Warm the wraps in a hot dry frying pan for 1 minute on each side, then remove and put on serving plates.

2 Spread the Hummus in a line down the centre of each wrap, top with 1 cos lettuce leaf, broken in half, then add a spoonful of Tomato & Coriander Salsa, 2 long strips of pickled cucumber, then, finally, top with a couple of spoonfuls of the hot beef casserole.

3 Fold the ends of the wrap inwards, then use a sheet of non-stick baking paper to roll the wrap up tightly. The paper helps keep the wrap together. Tuck the ends of the paper in like a parcel, then cut the wrap in half, with the paper still in place, to serve.

SOUPS

SERVES 4
PREP: 10 MINUTES
COOK: 50 MINUTES

CHICKPEA & CHORIZO SOUP

2 tbsp olive oil

2 onions, finely chopped

4 garlic cloves, finely chopped

150g/5½oz piece chorizo sausage, sliced

300g/10oz baking potatoes, peeled and diced

1 x 400g/14oz can chickpeas, drained

½ tsp hot paprika or chilli powder

1 litre/1¾ pints chicken or vegetable stock

sea salt and freshly ground black pepper

warm bread, to serve

CHORIZO IS ONE OF THOSE INGREDIENTS THAT CAN TURN EVERYDAY MUNDANE INGREDIENTS INTO SOMETHING EXTRA SPECIAL. IT KEEPS IN THE FRIDGE FOR SEVERAL WEEKS AND MAKES A GREAT BASE FOR THIS HEARTY SOUP-CUM-STEW.

1 Heat the oil in a medium saucepan, add the onions and fry over a medium heat for 10 minutes, stirring from time to time, until just beginning to soften. Add the garlic, chorizo and potatoes and fry for a further 10 minutes until the onion and potatoes have been coloured with the juices from the chorizo.

2 Stir in the chickpeas and paprika or chilli powder, stock and a generous sprinkling of salt and pepper. Bring to the boil, then cover with a lid, lower the heat and simmer for 30 minutes, stirring from time to time.

3 Ladle into bowls and serve with warm bread.

SERVES 4
PREP: 15 MINUTES
COOK: 42 MINUTES

TOMATO SOUP
WITH PITTA BREAD CROÛTONS

1 tbsp olive oil

1 red onion, chopped

1 potato, peeled and diced

650g/1lb 7oz tomatoes, peeled and roughly chopped

4 garlic cloves, finely chopped

1 tbsp dried oregano

1 tbsp fresh thyme, chopped

750ml/1¼ pints good vegetable stock

1 tbsp tomato purée

2 tsp granulated sugar

sea salt and freshly ground black pepper

fresh basil leaves, to garnish

For the pitta bread croûtons:

2 Pitta Breads (see p.110), shop bought, cut into 2cm/¾in squares

2 tbsp olive oil

2 garlic cloves, finely chopped

1 tsp dried oregano

EVERY COUNTRY HAS A FAVOURITE VERSION OF TOMATO SOUP. WE LIKE OURS FLAVOURED WITH GARLIC, OREGANO AND THYME AND LEFT CHUNKY, BUT FOR THOSE SMOOTH OPERATORS OUT THERE, FEEL FREE TO BLITZ YOURS IN A FOOD PROCESSOR OR BLENDER BEFORE SERVING.

1 To make the soup, heat the oil in a large saucepan, add the onion and potato and cook over a medium heat for 10 minutes, stirring from time to time, until just beginning to soften and to turn pale golden.

2 Mix in the tomatoes, garlic, oregano and thyme and cook for 2–3 minutes, then add the stock, tomato purée, sugar and a generous sprinkling of salt and pepper. Bring to the boil, then cover with a lid, lower the heat and simmer for 30 minutes, stirring from time to time, until the tomatoes are pulpy.

3 For the croûtons, preheat the oven to 200°C/400°F/ Gas mark 6.

4 Put the Pitta Breads into a small roasting tin, drizzle with the oil, then sprinkle the garlic and oregano over. Gently turn the bread until evenly coated in the oil, then spread out into an even layer and bake for 8–10 minutes until crisp.

5 Roughly mash or purée the soup in a blender to taste, then reheat if needed. Ladle the soup into bowls, sprinkle with fresh basil and top with the warm croûtons.

COOK'S TIP

To make this soup creamy, add 100ml/3½fl oz single cream towards the end of cooking.

SPICY LENTIL SOUP

250g/9oz red or green lentils

2 tbsp olive oil

1 large fresh or dried bay leaf

3 garlic cloves, finely chopped

½–1 large red chilli, deseeded and finely chopped

1 large red onion, finely chopped

1 tsp ground cumin

1.2 litres/2 pints chicken or vegetable stock

sea salt and freshly ground black pepper

small handful of fresh coriander, chopped

warm bread, to serve

sour cream, to garnish

SERVES 4
PREP: 15 MINUTES
COOK: 16–26 MINUTES

MADE WITH JUST A FEW HUMBLE INGREDIENTS, THIS SOUP WILL ONLY BE AS GOOD AS THE STOCK THAT YOU USE. PREFERABLY HOMEMADE VEGETABLE OR CHICKEN STOCK BUT A GOOD LOW-SALT CUBE IS FINE, BUT IF YOU HAVE THE REMAINS OF A ROAST CHICKEN, SIMMER IT IN WATER WITH SOME ONIONS, CARROTS AND HERBS FOR AN HOUR OR SO, THEN STRAIN AND USE AS THE BASE FOR THIS COMFORTING SOUP.

1 Rinse the lentils well in cold water, then leave to drain in a sieve. Heat the oil in a medium saucepan, add the bay leaf, garlic and half the chilli and fry over a low heat for 1 minute to release the flavours. Stir in the onion and fry for 5 minutes, stirring from time to time, until softened.

2 Mix in the drained lentils and cook for 2 minutes. Add the cumin and season well with salt and pepper. Add the stock, then bring to the boil, cover with a lid, lower the heat and simmer for 10–15 minutes, topping up with extra stock or water, if needed, until the lentils are tender.

3 Stir in the chopped coriander, then taste and adjust the seasoning, mixing in the remaining chilli or adding extra salt and pepper. Ladle into bowls and serve with warm bread. Garnish with a dollop of sour cream in each bowl.

MIXED BEAN & BACON SOUP

1 tbsp olive oil

1 red onion, chopped

115g/4oz streaky bacon rashers, sliced

4 frankfurter sausages, sliced

2 smoked Kabanos Polish sausages, sliced

4 garlic cloves, crushed

2 carrots, thinly sliced

1 litre/1¾ pints chicken or vegetable stock

1 x 400g/14oz can kidney beans, drained

1 x 400g/14oz can butter beans, drained

1 x 400g/14oz can chickpeas, drained

1 x 415g/14½oz can baked beans

3 tbsp sweet mild paprika

sea salt and freshly ground black pepper

2 tbsp sunflower oil

2 tbsp plain flour

½ red pepper, cored, deseeded and diced

½ green pepper, cored, deseeded and diced

SERVES 8
PREP: 15 MINUTES
COOK: 25 MINUTES

RONEN: THIS IS ONE OF MY MUM'S MOST PRIZED RECIPES, TRIED AND TESTED IN THE RESTAURANTS. IF YOU HAVEN'T HAD TIME TO SHOP OR YOU'RE A BIT LOW ON FUNDS THEN TRY THIS MAIN COURSE SOUP MADE WITH CANNED BEANS, FRESH VEGGIES AND CHOPPED BACON, PEPPED UP WITH SWEET PAPRIKA. IF YOU LIKE A LITTLE CHILLI HEAT, THEN CHOOSE SMOKED HOT PAPRIKA, WHICH IS WIDELY AVAILABLE IN LARGER SUPERMARKETS.

1 Heat the oil in a medium saucepan, add the onion and fry for 5 minutes, stirring from time to time, until just beginning to soften. Mix in the bacon, frankfurters, Kabanos, garlic and carrots and cook for 5 minutes, or until the bacon is just beginning to turn golden and the carrots soften.

2 Stir in all the beans and stock, season with paprika and salt and pepper and bring to the boil, stirring. Cover with a lid, lower the heat and simmer for 10 minutes.

3 Meanwhile, in a separate saucepan, heat 2 tbsp sunflower oil, add the flour and stir until golden. Add to the simmering soup, stir for 2 minutes, then turn off the heat.

4 Finally, stir in the chopped peppers (they don't need to cook down, they should be crunchy), then ladle the soup into bowls and serve with warm bread.

JERUSALEM ARTICHOKE SOUP
WITH CHESTNUT CREAM

2 tbsp sunflower oil

1 large white onion, chopped

350g/12oz Jerusalem artichokes

sea salt and freshly ground
black pepper

4 garlic cloves, chopped

600ml/1 pint good vegetable stock

200g/7oz vacuum pack ready
prepared chestnuts

150ml/¼ pint whipping cream

handful fresh chives, snipped

SERVES 4
PREP: 20 MINUTES
COOK: 40 MINUTES

JERUSALEM ARTICHOKES DON'T LOOK VERY PROMISING BUT THEY MAKE THE MOST WONDERFUL VELVETY SMOOTH SOUP WITH A LIGHT DELICATE FLAVOUR ALL OF THEIR OWN. BLITZING READY PREPARED CHESTNUTS WITH CREAM ADDS A KIND OF GLAM TOPPING THAT TASTES FABULOUS SPOONED INTO THE CENTRE OF THE SOUP BEFORE BEING TOPPED WITH SOME EXTRA CRUMBLED CHESTNUTS OR SNIPPED FRESH CHIVES.

1 Heat the oil in a medium saucepan, add the onion and fry for 5 minutes over a low heat, stirring from time to time, until softened but not browned.

2 Meanwhile, peel and slice the Jerusalem artichokes. They discolour quickly so do this at the very last minute, then rinse with cold water, drain and slice. Add the artichokes to the onion with a pinch of salt and fry over a low heat for 5 minutes, stirring from time to time, until just beginning to soften.

3 Stir in the garlic, then pour in the stock and bring to the boil, stirring. Cover with a lid, lower the heat and simmer for 20–30 minutes until the artichokes are tender.

4 Meanwhile, crush half the chestnuts with a stick blender or fork and gradually stir into the cream until smooth. Spoon into a bowl and chill until needed.

5 Blitz the soup still in the pan with a stick blender or transfer to a blender and blend. Taste and adjust the seasoning if needed, then reheat and ladle into small bowls. Add a spoonful of the chestnut cream to the centre of each and top with a few remaining chestnuts, crumbled into small pieces. Some snipped fresh chives also work well as a garnish.

SALADS

ROASTED AUBERGINE SALAD

3 large aubergines
1 lemon, halved
salt
Tahini Sauce (see p.98)
chopped fresh parsley, for sprinkling
olive oil, for drizzling

For the Dip (optional):

3 large aubergines
1 red pepper, halved, deseeded and finely diced
3 fresh thyme sprigs, leaves only (to give about 1 tbsp)
3 tbsp chopped fresh oregano or ¼ tsp dried
sea salt and freshly ground black pepper
2 tbsp olive oil
juice of ½ lemon
2 tbsp Tahini Sauce (see p.98)

To garnish:

½ pomegranate, seeds removed from casing (optional)
3 tbsp chopped fresh flat-leaf parsley

To serve:

warm Pitta Breads (see p.110)
pepper, carrot and cucumber sticks

SERVES 4
PREP: 15 MINUTES
COOK:
30–40 MINUTES

YOU CAN EAT THIS WITH TAHINI (LEBANESE-STYLE), WITH YOGURT (TURKISH-STYLE), OR SIMPLY WITH LOTS OF LEMON AND A LITTLE GARLIC. OUR FAVOURITE IS WITH TAHINI – IT'S A MATCH MADE IN HEAVEN. IN THE MIDDLE EAST THE CHARRED AUBERGINES ARE SIMPLY THROWN DOWN INTO THE MIDDLE OF THE TABLE AND EVERYONE DIGS IN WITH THEIR SPOONS, FIGHTING FOR THE LAST PIECES OF SUCCULENT FLESH. WE HAVE ALSO ADDED A VARIATION TO TURN THE COOKED AUBERGINE INTO A BABA GANOUSH–STYLE DIP TO SERVE AS PART OF A MEZZE SPREAD.

1 Char the aubergines directly over a hob gas flame. No need for a rack; just put them straight on the top with the heat set to medium. Cook for 15-20 minutes, turning with tongs as the skin blackens, cracks and white ash spots begin to appear, until the skin is the same all over. They will puff up as they cook and some steam may escape, so pay attention and don't over-burn them. If you don't have a gas hob, preheat the grill to high. Remove the grill rack and cook the aubergines directly in the pan, checking that they are about 3cm/1in away from the heat source. Grill for 30-45 minutes, turning them several times until the skin is blackened and papery and beginning to turn ash white.

2 Transfer the hot aubergines to a chopping board or large plate, make a slit along the lengths and open out. Squeeze in the lemon juice, flavour with a little salt, LOTS of Tahini Sauce, a little parsley, then drizzle with olive oil. Give guests teaspoons to scoop the delicious warm flesh from the skins. Don't worry if you eat the skin – it all adds to the amazing flavour. One lucky guest can bite into the head of the aubergine to extract the best part.

3 To make the Baba Ganoush Dip, cook the aubergines as above, then leave to cool. When completely cold, slit in half, scoop the flesh out, then roughly chop. Add to a bowl, stir in the diced red pepper, thyme, oregano and salt and pepper to taste. Drizzle with the oil, lemon juice and Tahini Sauce to taste, then toss gently together. Garnish with pomegranate seeds and parsley and serve with pitta and pepper, carrot and cucumber sticks.

SERVES 4
PREP: 15 MINUTES
COOK: 1 HOUR

ROASTED VEGETABLE SALAD

2 large red onions, about 250g/9oz, cut into large chunks

2 sweet potatoes, about 650g/1lb 7oz, peeled and cut into chunks about 2.5cm/1in

3 tbsp light muscovado sugar

2 garlic cloves, roughly chopped

4 tbsp olive oil

sea salt and freshly ground black pepper

½ small white cabbage, about 350g/12oz, cut into large chunks

2 courgettes, about 400g/14oz, cut into large chunks

25g/1oz fresh flat-leaf parsley, roughly chopped

125ml/4fl oz Yellow Sauce (see p.106)

THIS VERY SLOW ROASTED MIX OF RED ONION, SWEET POTATO AND COURGETTE HAS A SURPRISE ADDITION OF WHITE CABBAGE – NOT NORMALLY AN INGREDIENT YOU THINK OF TO ROAST, BUT IT WORKS WELL IN A WINTERY SALAD SPRINKLED WITH LOTS OF CHOPPED PARSLEY AND SERVED WITH OUR SERIOUSLY GARLICKY SAUCE ON P.106.

1 Preheat the oven to 150°C/300°F/Gas mark 2.

2 Put the red onions and sweet potatoes into a roasting tin. Sprinkle with the sugar and half the garlic, then drizzle with 2 tablespoons of the oil and season with salt and pepper. Using your hands, toss the vegetables in the oil and sugar mix until they are evenly coated.

3 Put the white cabbage and courgettes into a separate roasting tin, sprinkle with the remaining garlic, and olive oil, then add salt and pepper and mix together.

4 Roast all the vegetables for about 1 hour, turning once or twice, until they are soft and very lightly browned. Take out of the oven and leave to cool.

5 Transfer the roasted vegetables to a serving bowl, sprinkle with the chopped parsley and spoon over the Yellow Sauce.

TABOULEH

PACKED WITH CHOPPED MINT AND PARSLEY (YOU'RE AIMING FOR HALF HERBS TO BULGHUR), THIS LEMONY DRESSED BULGHUR OR CRACKED WHEAT SALAD IS GREAT SERVED WITH VIRTUALLY ANY SAVOURY MAIN DISH, OR AS A SIMPLE STARTER WITH BABY COS LETTUCE LEAVES TO SCOOP IT UP.

100g/3½oz fine grade bulghur wheat

4 tbsp virgin olive oil

juice of 1 lemon

sea salt and freshly ground black pepper

25g/1oz fresh mint, finely chopped

55g/2oz fresh flat-leaf parsley

2 plum tomatoes, finely diced

¼ cucumber, diced

½ bunch of spring onions, finely chopped

½ pomegranate, seeds removed from casing

1 Tip the bulghur wheat into a bowl, cover with cold salted water and leave to soak for at least 30 minutes until softened.

2 Drain the bulghur wheat if required and spoon into a salad bowl, then pour over the dressing and stir together.

3 Add the chopped herbs, tomatoes, cucumber and spring onions to the bulhur wheat, stirring gently.

4 Using a fork, stir the oil, lemon juice and a generous sprinkling of salt and pepper together in a small bowl. Only add the dressing just as you are about to serve., scattering the pomegranate seeds on top.

SERVES 4
PREP: 15 MINUTES
SOAK: 30 MINUTES
COOK: 10 MINUTES

MIXED VEGETABLE SALAD

1 red pepper, halved, cored, deseeded and cut into 2cm/¾in dice

½ cucumber, skin partly peeled, halved and deseeded if liked, then cut into 2cm/¾in dice

225g/8oz cherry tomatoes on the vine, halved

For the dressing:
small bunch of fresh flat-leaf parsley, about 15g/½oz, finely chopped

1 garlic clove, finely chopped

2 tbsp white wine vinegar

2 tbsp olive oil

1 tbsp runny honey

1 tsp granulated sugar

sea salt and coarsely ground black pepper

YOU CAN TRANSFORM THESE EVERYDAY VEGETABLES INTO A COLOURFUL SIDE DISH WITH THIS TANGY DRESSING. WHEN WE MAKE UP LARGE QUANTITIES OF THE DRESSING FOR THE RESTAURANT WE BLITZ THE INGREDIENTS IN A BLENDER. HOWEVER, THIS DOMESTIC QUANTITY MAY BE TOO SMALL FOR YOUR PROCESSOR, BUT IF YOU HAVE A MINI BOWL OR SPICE MILL ATTACHMENT THEN THIS WOULD WORK FINE. UNLIKE LETTUCE-BASED SALADS, THIS ONE TASTES JUST AS GOOD THE NEXT DAY, SO IT'S GREAT TO PACK INTO A SMALL POT FOR LUNCHBOXES, KEEPING THE DRESSING ON THE SIDE.

1 Put the red pepper, cucumber and tomatoes into a salad bowl and toss together.

2 For the dressing, add the parsley to a bowl with the garlic, vinegar and oil. Mix in the honey and sugar, then generously season with salt and pepper. Alternatively, blitz in a blender or spice mill.

3 Spoon the dressing over the salad and toss together gently before serving.

SERVES 4
PREP: 15 MINUTES

FALAFEL SALAD

oil, for deep-frying

1 quantity shaped but uncooked Falafel (see p.19)

400g/14oz white cabbage, finely shredded

½ cos lettuce, leaves separated and shredded

salt

1 quantity Tomato & Coriander Salsa (see p.103)

1 quantity Tzatziki (see p.102)

2 tbsp olive oil, for drizzling

FALAFELS ARE VERY MOORISH, BUT THEY'RE FRIED, SO NEED TO BE BALANCED IN A SALAD. HERE WE BALANCE THEIR TEXTURE AND TASTE BY ADDING CABBAGE FOR CRUNCH, TOMATOES FOR ACIDITY, CORIANDER FOR FRESHNESS AND TZATZIKI TO OFFSET THE OIL. YOU WON'T FIND THIS COMBINATION ELSEWHERE (AS IT'S NOT A TRADITIONAL WAY TO EAT FALAFEL) BUT WE THINK IT WORKS.

1 Heat the oil for deep-frying in a pan to 180°C/350°F (a square of day-old bread should immediately sizzle in it). Lower 3 Falafel into the oil and cook for 3–4 minutes until golden on the outside but so that you can still see the green of the herbs. Remove with a slotted spoon to a plate lined with kitchen paper. Test that they are done by cutting one in half; they should be cooked through and light and fluffy on the inside. Continue frying the Falafel in batches, checking the temperature of the oil from time to time.

2 Divide the shredded white cabbage and lettuce between the plates, season with salt, then top with spoonfuls of the salsa and Tzatziki. Drizzle with a little olive oil, then arrange the Falafel on the Tzatziki and serve.

SERVES 4
PREP: 15 MINUTES
COOK: 10 MINUTES

GREEK SALAD

1 red or green pepper, halved, deseeded and diced

½ cucumber, partly peeled, deseeded if liked and diced

200g/7oz cherry tomatoes on the vine, halved

1 red onion, thinly sliced

100g/3½oz feta cheese, drained

¼ tsp dried oregano

3 tbsp olive oil

A CLASSIC AND ALL-TIME FAVOURITE, THIS SALAD IS FRESH TASTING, CRISP, CRUNCHY AND PRETTY CHUNKY, TOO. GREEKS PUT A SLAB OF FETA ON TOP OF THE SALAD, BUT WE FIND THAT CRUMBLING THE FETA HELPS IT REACH ALL PARTS OF THE SALAD AND MAKES IT BETTER FOR SHARING. FETA IS QUITE SALTY, SO THERE'S NO NEED TO ADD EXTRA SALT – JUST SEASON WITH LOTS OF DRIED OREGANO.

FOR AN ADDED DIMENSION, TRY ADDING SOME CAPERS AND CAPER LEAVES.

1 Put the green pepper, cucumber, tomatoes and onion into a salad bowl and toss together gently. Crumble the feta into small pieces with your fingertips or dice if you prefer. Sprinkle over the salad with the dried oregano, then drizzle with the oil and serve.

SERVES 4
PREP: 15 MINUTES

FATOUSH

For the pitta bread croûtons:
2 Pitta Breads (see p.110) or shop bought

2–3 tbsp olive oil

up to 2 tsp Za'atar Spice Blend if made with dried herbs or 2 tbsp if made with fresh herbs (see below)

For the salad:
1 small iceberg lettuce, cut into bite-sized pieces

1 green pepper, halved, cored, deseeded and diced

½ bunch of spring onions, thinly sliced

¼ cucumber, diced

2 tomatoes, diced

handful of fresh parsley, finely chopped

handful of fresh mint, finely chopped

For the dressing:
4 tbsp olive oil

juice of 1 lemon

1 tsp sumac seeds, finely crushed

sea salt and freshly ground black pepper

SERVES 4
PREP: 15 MINUTES
COOK: 30–35 MINUTES

THIS CRISP CRUNCHY SALAD IS A GREAT WAY TO USE UP THOSE LAST ONE OR TWO PITTA BREADS THAT YOU MIGHT HAVE LEFT OVER. BAKE THEM IN THE OVEN UNTIL CRISP AND THEN FINISH WITH A DRIZZLE OF OLIVE OIL AND ZA'ATAR SPICES – A POPULAR SPICE MIX MADE WITH THYME, OREGANO AND OUR FAVOURITE SESAME SEEDS.

1 Preheat the oven to 150°C/300°F/Gas mark 2.

2 Cut the Pitta Breads into 2cm/¾in squares, scatter over a baking sheet, then drizzle with the oil and sprinkle with the za'atar. Bake for 25–30 minutes, checking every 10 minutes or so, turning the squares and moving them around so that they all dry out evenly.

3 Meanwhile, put all the salad ingredients into a large salad bowl and toss together gently.

4 Put all the dressing ingredients into a small jug and stir together with a fork. Alternatively, put everything in a jam jar, screw on the lid and shake to mix.

5 Pour the dressing over the salad and toss gently together. Sprinkle over the hot croûtons and serve immediately.

ZA'ATAR SPICE BLEND

Toast 1 tablespoon of sesame seeds in a dry frying pan until just beginning to brown, then pound with a pestle in a mortar. Mix in 1 teaspoon each of dried thyme and oregano and ½ teaspoon of salt. This mix will keep in a jam jar in the fridge for up to a month.

SERVES 4
PREP: 15 MINUTES
COOK: 10 MINUTES

CAULIFLOWER WITH GREEN TAHINI

1 large cauliflower (or 2 small ones)

40g/1½oz fresh flat-leaf parsley, finely chopped

2 large garlic cloves, finely chopped

300g/10oz Tahini Sauce (see p.98)

1 litre/1¾ pints rapeseed oil, for deep-frying

1 lemon, cut into wedges

salt

THE BRITISH GROW LOTS OF CAULIFLOWERS, BUT IT IS ONE OF THOSE INGREDIENTS THAT IS RARELY SERVED AND WHEN IT'S COOKED, TENDS JUST TO BE PLAIN BOILED OR SMOTHERED IN CHEESE SAUCE. THIS SALAD OF CRISPY DEEP-FRIED CAULIFLOWER FLORETS, SERVED ON A BED OF PARSLEY-SPECKLED GARLIC TAHINI SAUCE, LIFTS THIS HUMBLE VEGGIE TO A WHOLE NEW LEVEL.

1 Cut any leaves from the cauliflower, cut in half and then cut away the florets and discard the woody core. Cut any larger florets into even bite-sized florets so they will all cook in the same time.

2 Stir the parsley and garlic into the Tahini Sauce and set aside.

3 Pour the oil for deep-frying into a medium saucepan so that the pan is only half full, then heat the oil to 160°C/325°F. Alternatively, test by adding a cauliflower floret to the hot oil; the oil should immediately sizzle around the cauliflower when it is hot enough.

4 Add the cauliflower to the hot oil, a few pieces at a time, until about one-third of the florets are in the oil. Don't overcrowd the pan or the oil temperature will drop too much. Deep-fry for 2–3 minutes until the cauliflower is browned, then scoop out of the pan with a slotted spoon and transfer to a plate lined with kitchen paper. Bring the oil back to temperature, then continue cooking the cauliflower in small batches until all the florets are done. Leave to cool for a few minutes.

5 Spoon the Tahini Sauce over 4 serving plates, then top with the cauliflower. Squeeze over a little lemon juice and salt to taste and serve immediately. Alternatively, serve in separate bowls for your guests to mix themselves.

BREADS AND SAUCES

TAHINI SAUCE

175g/6oz tahini (just over half a 340g/12oz jar)

2 tbsp freshly squeezed lemon juice, plus extra to serve

sea salt, to taste

125ml/4fl oz cold water

To serve:

1 quantity Green Chilli Sauce (see p.104)

4 Pitta Breads (see p.110), warmed and cut into strips

SERVES 4
MAKES 300G/10½OZ
PREP: 10 MINUTES

TAHINI IS THE BASIS TO ALL LEVANTINE CUISINE AND IS AVAILABLE IN JARS FROM HEALTH FOOD SHOPS AND SOME LARGER SUPERMARKETS. MAKE SURE YOU MASTER THE BASIC ART OF HANDLING THIS INGREDIENT – IT BEHAVES LIKE QUICKSAND AT FIRST, SO READ THE INSTRUCTIONS CAREFULLY. OUR FAVOURITE WAY TO SERVE THIS DELICIOUS SAUCE IS AS AN APPETISER SPREAD OVER SMALL PLATES, DRIZZLED WITH GREEN CHILLI SAUCE (P.104) AND A SQUEEZE OF EXTRA FRESH LEMON JUICE WITH WARM PITTA BREADS (P.110) TO SCOOP IT UP.

1 Put the tahini, lemon juice and salt to taste into a bowl and gradually mix in the cold water with a wooden whisk or spoon. The mixture will behave a little like quicksand and become firmer the more water you add. While it is still quite hard, taste it to see whether it needs more lemon or salt and add if necessary.

2 Continue slowly adding the water. When almost all the water is added the tahini will start to soften as it becomes saturated but will still be a thick spreadable paste rather like softly whipped cream.

2 Spoon on to small serving plates, spread into an even layer with the back of a spoon, then drizzle with Green Chilli Sauce and serve with warm Pitta Bread strips.

VARIATION

For green tahini sauce, stir 2 finely chopped garlic cloves and 6 tablespoons chopped fresh parsley into the recipe left.

SERVES 4–6
PREP: 10 MINUTES

GUACAMOLE

2 avocados, halved, stoned, peeled and cut into 1cm/½in dice

2 plum tomatoes, halved and finely chopped

½ red pepper, cored, deseeded and finely chopped

½ red onion, finely chopped

2 spring onions, finely chopped

small bunch of fresh flat-leaf parsley, or coriander finely chopped

2 tbsp olive oil

juice of 1 lemon

sea salt and freshly ground black pepper

To serve (optional):

450g/1lb Hummus (see p.19)

paprika, for sprinkling

fresh parsley, chopped, to garnish

AVOCADOS GO BROWN EVEN WHEN TOSSED IN LEMON JUICE, SO IF YOU WANT TO MAKE THIS IN ADVANCE, MIX ALL THE VEGGIES AND DRESSING TOGETHER, THEN PREPARE AND ADD THE AVOCADO AT THE VERY LAST MINUTE. WE PREFER CHUNKY DICED AVOCADO RATHER THAN THE MORE USUAL MASHED VERSION AND WE HOPE YOU DO, TOO.

Put the avocados, tomatoes, red pepper, red onion and spring onions into a bowl. Sprinkle over the parsley and gently toss together. Drizzle over the oil and lemon juice, season to taste, then gently toss together. Serve immediately. We like it on a bed of Hummus, sprinkled with a little paprika and extra chopped fresh parsley.

TZATZIKI

1 cucumber
¼ tsp sea salt
250g/9oz Greek yogurt
1 garlic clove, crushed
freshly ground black pepper
olive oil, for drizzling

PRONOUNCED "DZA-DZI-KI", THIS IS WONDERFULLY COOLING AND REFRESHING, AND IS A GREAT ADDED EXTRA TO WRAPS, OR TO TOP SPICED MEATS OR VEGGIES. SALTING THE CUCUMBER IS A NATURAL WAY OF MAKING SURE THERE'S ENOUGH (BUT NOT TOO MUCH) SALT IN THE DISH. THE SALTED CUCUMBER "SWEATS" OUT EXCESS SALT AND WATER, LEAVING YOU WITH LOVELY SALTY CUCUMBER FLESH AND AS LITTLE LIQUID AS POSSIBLE. THE DIP WILL KEEP FOR 3-4 DAYS IN THE FRIDGE.

SERVES 6
MAKES: 500G/ILB 2OZ
PREP: 10 MINUTES
STAND: 30 MINUTES-
1 HOUR

1 Cut the cucumber in half lengthways, then scoop out the seeds with a teaspoon. Finely chop the flesh, then put into a sieve and set this over a bowl. Sprinkle the salt over the cucumber and leave to stand for 30 minutes-1 hour to allow the salt to draw out some of the juices and to drain into the bowl.

2 Put the yogurt, garlic and a little pepper into a mixing bowl and stir together. Add the cucumber, mix together, then spoon into a serving dish. Drizzle a little olive oil on top to serve.

TOMATO & CORIANDER SALSA

1 red onion, quartered

½–1 large green chilli, quartered and deseeded

25g/1oz fresh coriander

250g/9oz vine tomatoes, quartered, deseeded and chopped finely

2 tbsp olive oil

sea salt and freshly ground black pepper

SERVES 6
MAKES: 450G/ILB
PREP: IO MINUTES

HOW HOT YOU MAKE THIS IS VERY MUCH DOWN TO YOU AND THE KIND OF CHILLIES THAT YOU USE. WE PREFER TO BUY THE LARGE FINGER CHILLIES AND TO TAKE THE SEEDS OUT. START WITH HALF A CHOPPED CHILLI, AS YOU CAN ALWAYS ADD EXTRA IF YOU WANT TO CRANK THE HEAT UP A BIT.

1 Put the onion, half the green chilli and the coriander into a food processor and finely chop. Spoon into a serving bowl. Add the chopped tomatoes, then stir in the oil and ¼ teaspoon salt, pepper to taste. Alternatively, finely chop all the vegetables on a chopping board and mix with the salt, pepper and oil in a bowl.

2 Taste the salsa and gradually stir in the remaining chilli, finely chopped, as needed.

GREEN CHILLI SAUCE

115g/4oz large long green chillies, halved, deseeded and cut into chunks

115g/4oz plum tomatoes, peeled if liked and cut into chunks

25g/1oz fresh coriander, including the leaves and stalks

25g/1oz (about 4) large garlic cloves, sliced

1 tsp coriander seeds, roughly crushed

2 tsp granulated sugar

¼ tsp sea salt and freshly ground black pepper

SERVES 4–6
MAKES: 250ML/
9FL OZ
PREP: 10 MINUTES

DON'T THINK YOU'RE WIMPING OUT BY TAKING OUT THE CHILLI SEEDS, THIS SAUCE IS PLENTY HOT AND POKEY WITHOUT THEM. OF COURSE, IF YOUR CHILLIES ARE VERY MILD, THEN LEAVE THE SEEDS IN. ADD JUST A TEASPOON OR TWO OF THIS TO ANY DISH, BUT IT'S ESPECIALLY NICE WITH BARBECUED AUBERGINES, TAHINI SAUCE AND HUMMUS – ITS SMOKIN! FOR BEST RESULTS, ALWAYS ENHACE WITH A LITTLE LEMON JUICE JUST BEFORE SERVING.

Put all the ingredients into a blender or food processor and blitz until a coarse paste forms Spoon into a small bowl or a Le Parfait-style clip jar and store in the fridge. It will keep for at least a week.

YELLOW SAUCE

1 large garlic bulb, about 70 g/2½oz, separated into cloves, smashed with a knife, peeled and halved

6 tbsp olive oil

3 fresh thyme sprigs, leaves only, to give about 1 tbsp

2 fresh sage sprigs, leaves only

85g/3oz granulated sugar

juice of 1 lemon

sea salt and freshly ground black pepper

SERVES 6
MAKES: 175ML/6FL OZ
PREP: 10 MINUTES
COOK: 5 MINUTES

THIS SAUCE IS SERIOUSLY GARLICKY, SO A LITTLE GOES A LONG WAY. ALTHOUGH IT'S VERY GARLICKY IT IS TEMPERED WITH THE SWEET AND SOUR BALANCE OF SUGAR AND LEMON JUICE AND SPECKLED GREEN WITH FRESH THYME AND SAGE LEAVES. IT COMPLEMENTS THE ROASTED VEGETABLE SALAD ON P.84. ANY LEFTOVERS CAN BE KEPT IN A SCREW-TOPPED JAR IN THE FRIDGE AND CAN BE USED AS AN EASY SALAD DRESSING OR TO LIFT BRUSCHETTA-STYLE GRILLED TOMATOES ON TOASTED CIABATTA OR SOURDOUGH FOR A QUICK LUNCH.

1 Put the garlic into a small saucepan, pour in half the oil and cook over a low heat for 5 minutes until the garlic is just turning pale golden brown. Remove from the heat, add the herbs, sugar and lemon juice and stir until the sugar has dissolved.

2 Transfer to a blender or a small food processor and blitz until smooth. Alternatively, use a stick blender in the pan. Stir in the remaining oil and add salt and pepper to taste.

3 Pour into a jam jar and screw on the lid. This will keep for 2–3 days in the fridge.

108

GARLIC & LEMON SAUCE

juice of 3 lemons
3 garlic cloves, very finely chopped
2 pickled chilli peppers, drained and finely chopped
sea salt and freshly ground black pepper

To serve:
Hummus (see p.19)
warm Pitta Breads (see p.110)

THIS IS A MIXTURE THAT ADDS A DIFFERENT DIMENSION TO ANY HUMMUS DISH. WE DON'T PUT GARLIC IN OUR HUMMUS (SOME CUSTOMERS DON'T WANT GARLIC BREATH, SO THIS GIVES THEM AN OPTION) BUT WE LOVE DRIZZLING THIS SAUCE OVER THE TOP – THE ACID FROM THE LEMONS TOGETHER WITH THE BITTERNESS OF THE GARLIC AND SPICED SALTINESS OF THE PICKLED CHILLIES MAKE IT IRRESISTIBLE.

1 Put all the ingredients into a bowl and, using a fork, stir together to mix. Alternatively, put in a jam jar, screw on the lid and shake well.

2 Leave to stand for 30 minutes or so for the flavours to develop, then strain. Drizzle over plates of Hummus and serve with warm Pitta Breads.

COOK'S TIP

SAVE TIME AND AVOID GARLICKY SCENTED FINGERS BY BLITZING ALL THE SAUCE INGREDIENTS TOGETHER IN A LIQUIDISER RATHER THAN CHOPPING BY HAND.

WHOLEMEAL PITTA BREAD

140g/5oz wholemeal flour
250g/9oz strong white bread flour, plus extra for dusting
1 tsp sea salt
1 tsp caster sugar
2 tsp easy-blend dried yeast
250ml/8fl oz warm water
oil, for oiling

DRIED EASY-BLEND YEAST MAKES BREAD-MAKING SUPER EASY, AS THERE'S NO WAITING AND FROTHING OF YEAST. JUST STIR IT INTO THE FLOUR WITH THE WARM WATER AND AWAY YOU GO. THE OVEN TEMPERATURE MIGHT SEEM LOWER THAN FOR MOST BREADS BUT IT REALLY DOES WORK. IF YOU HAVE A GLASS OVEN DOOR, THE KIDS WILL LOVE TO WATCH THE BREADS PUFF UP MAGICALLY IN THE OVEN.

1 Put the flours, salt and sugar into an electric mixer, then sprinkle over the yeast and stir together. With the machine running, gradually mix in enough of the warm water until a soft dough is formed, then beat for 5 minutes on low speed.

2 Increase the machine speed and mix for a further 5 minutes to develop the gluten and until the dough is silky smooth and elastic. If you don't have a mixer, then make the dough in a bowl with a wooden spoon and knead on a lightly floured work surface for as long as your muscles will let you.

3 Transfer the dough to a lightly oiled bowl, cover the top with oiled clingfilm and put in a warm place for 30 minutes until the dough is almost twice the size.

4 Knead the dough once more but this time just for a few minutes. Cut into 8 pieces, then roll out each piece to a round, about 13–15 cm/5–6in in diameter. Place on lightly floured baking sheets and cover once more with oiled clingfilm. Leave to rise for 30 minutes. Meanwhile, preheat the oven to 180°C/350°F/ Gas mark 4.

5 Take off the clingfilm and bake the breads for 3–5 minutes until puffed up and just beginning to tinge brown. Remove and wrap in a clean tea towel to keep them soft. Serve warm, split and filled or reheat cold pittas on a preheated griddle pan for 2–3 minutes or under a hot grill.

MAKES 8
PREP: 25 MINUTES
RISE: 1 HOUR
COOK: 3–5 MINUTES

FLATBREAD WITH ZA'ATAR

500g/1lb 2oz white bread flour, plus a little extra for dusting

1 tsp salt

2 tsp easy-blend dried yeast

2 tsp runny honey

4 tbsp olive oil, plus extra for oiling and drizzling

300ml/½ pint warm water

1 tbsp Za'atar Spice Blend (see p.92)

2 tbsp sesame seeds

MAKES: 2 LARGE BREADS
PREP: 30 MINUTES
RISE: 1½ HOURS
COOK: 15–20 MINUTES

VERSIONS OF THIS FLATBREAD CAN BE FOUND ALL OVER THE MIDDLE EAST AND SERVED FOR BREAKFAST OR AS PART OF A MEZZE. BREAK THROUGH THE FRAGRANT CRISP ZA'ATAR AND SESAME CRUST TO THE SOFT DOUGH BENEATH. MAKING YOUR OWN BREAD IS WONDERFULLY RELAXING, BUT THE HARDEST PART IS WAITING FOR IT TO BE COOL ENOUGH TO EAT!

1 Put the flour, salt and yeast into a large mixing bowl and stir together. Add the honey and 2 tablespoons of the oil and gradually mix in enough warm water with a wooden spoon, then mix with your hands to make a soft but not sticky dough. You may not need all of the water.

2 Knead the dough for 5 minutes until smooth and elastic. Alternatively, mix and knead in an electric mixer with a dough hook, if you have one.

3 Put the dough into a large lightly oiled bowl, cover with oiled clingfilm and then leave in a warm place for 45–60 minutes, or until the dough has doubled in size.

4 Punch the dough down with a fist, then scoop out of the bowl and knead well on a lightly floured work surface for 2–3 minutes until smooth again. Cut the dough in half and roll each half out to a round, about 23cm/9in in diameter. Put each on to an oiled baking sheet.

5 Slash the top of each bread with criss-cross lines, brush with the remaining oil, then sprinkle with the za'atar and sesame seeds. Cover the top of each bread loosely with oiled clingfilm and leave to rise for 30 minutes. Meanwhile, preheat the oven to 230°C/425°F/Gas mark 7.

6 Take off the clingfilm and bake the breads for 15–20 minutes, swapping oven positions around after 10 minutes so that they brown evenly. Cook until golden brown and the bread sounds hollow when tapped with your fingertips. Drizzle with a little extra olive oil. Transfer to a wire rack to cool, then break into pieces to serve.

COOK'S TIP

IF YOU DON'T THINK YOU WILL BE ABLE TO EAT BOTH BREADS, THEN WRAP ONE IN CLINGFILM WHEN COMPLETELY COLD, SEAL, LABEL AND FREEZE FOR UP TO A MONTH. DEFROST AT ROOM TEMPERATURE, THEN UNWRAP AND WARM IN A LOW OVEN BEFORE SERVING.

LABANEH
(SOUR YOGURT CHEESE)

1.5kg/3lb 5oz natural yogurt with 4.2% fat content

1 tsp fine grain salt

To serve:

olive oil, for drizzling
Za'atar Spice Blend (see p.92)
warm Pitta Breads (see p.110)

RONEN: I LOVE TO EAT LABANEH SPREAD ON PAPER-THIN DRUZE PITTA BREAD WITH ZA'ATAR AND PICKLED OREGANO LEAVES. MY SISTER'S GIRLS ARE ALSO HUGE FANS – A SANDWICH WITH LABANEH IS THEIR PREFERRED LUNCH ALL WEEK LONG.

IT'S THE ULTIMATE SIMPLE FOOD AS IT'S EASY TO MAKE AND EFFORTLESS TO SERVE. SIMPLY STIR SOME SALT INTO YOGURT AND LEAVE TO DRIP TIED IN MUSLIN FOR 8–12 HOURS, OR OVERNIGHT. IF YOU TIE THE BAG OVER THE TAP BEFORE YOU GO TO BED THE YOGURT CAN DRIP STRAIGHT INTO THE SINK, THEN YOU CAN TRANSFER IT TO THE FRIDGE THE NEXT MORNING. THE LONGER YOU LEAVE IT, THE DENSER THE CHEESE WILL BE.

LABANEH IS IDEAL AS PART OF A MEZZE. IT CAN ALSO BE SHAPED INTO SMALL BALLS AND KEPT IN A JAR OF OLIVE OIL TO PROLONG ITS KEEPING

SERVES 8–10
MAKES 550G/1LB 4OZ
PREP: 10 MINUTES
STAND: 8–12 HOURS, OR OVERNIGHT

1 Put a large square of muslin that is at least 38cm/15in square into a mixing bowl. Pour over boiling water and leave to soak for 3–4 minutes to sterilise it. Remove with tongs, then drape the muslin over a colander set over a second smaller bowl.

2 Drain the water from the bowl, dry and add the yogurt and salt. Stir together, then spoon into the muslin-lined colander. Bring the edges of the muslin together over the yogurt, twist and tie with string and make a loop long enough to hook over the kitchen tap. Alternatively, tie it from the knob of a high kitchen cupboard or use a preserving jelly stand if you have one. Make sure you have a bowl under the bag to catch the liquid; it will run out quickly and look white and milky to begin with, then after 10 minutes will begin to drip clear liquid. Leave for 8–12 hours, or overnight until firm.

3 Transfer the muslin bag of cheese to a plate. Chill in the fridge until required, then peel away the muslin, put on a board and serve drizzled with olive oil and za'atar spice mix with warm Pitta Breads as part of a mezze-style mix of dishes.

COOK'S TIP

DON'T BE TEMPTED TO USE FAT-FREE YOGURT, AS YOU NEED THE FAT FOR THE BEST TASTE!

DESSERTS

MALABI

55g/2oz cornflour
600ml/1 pint full-fat milk
100ml/3½fl oz double cream
100g/3½oz granulated sugar
3 tbsp runny date honey

To decorate:
fresh baby mint leaves
pomegranate seeds (optional)

SERVES 6
PREP: 10 MINUTES
COOK: 5 MINUTES
SET: 3-4 HOURS

MALABI OR MUHALLABIEH IS A MILK PUDDING THICKENED WITH CORNFLOUR. OK, SO THEY DON'T SOUND TERRIBLY THRILLING, BUT THESE ARE PUDDINGS WE HAVE GROWN UP WITH. THINK OF THEM LIKE PANNA COTTA BUT WITHOUT THE GELATINE. WHAT LIFTS THESE DESSERTS INTO ANOTHER REALM IS THE SYRUP THAT YOU ADD JUST BEFORE SERVING – A GENEROUS DRIZZLE OF DARK DATE HONEY IS OUR ALL-TIME FAVOURITE.

1 Put the cornflour into a bowl and gradually mix in about one-third of the milk to make a smooth paste.

2 Pour the rest of the milk into a medium saucepan, add the cream and sugar and heat gently so that the sugar dissolves. When the creamy milk mixture begins to get hot and release steam, gradually stir in the cornflour paste with a wooden spoon. Continue heating the milk mix until it is brought to the boil. Check the temperature with a sugar thermometer. As soon as it reaches 95°C/203°F the mix will begin to thicken. Remove from the heat immediately.

3 Pour into 6 damp 150ml/ ¼ pint individual pudding moulds and leave to cool at room temperature. Cover the tops with clingfilm and chill in the fridge for 3 hours, longer if you have the time so that the puddings can set firm.

4 When you are ready to serve, loosen the edges of the malabi with a damp knife, then turn them out on to small curved plates. Drizzle the date honey over the puddings and decorate with fresh mint leaves and pomegranate seeds.

SERVES 6
PREP: 15 MINUTES
COOK: 16–18 MINUTES

GLUTEN-FREE CHOCOLATE BROWNIES

40g/1½oz butter, plus extra
for greasing

300g/10½oz dark chocolate, broken
into pieces

175g/6oz granulated sugar

150ml/¼ pint double cream

3 eggs, separated

To serve:

sifted icing sugar

few sliced pistachio nuts

salted cashew or vanilla ice cream
(optional)

IT'S HARD TO RESIST THESE DARK, RICH, CHOCOLATE-PACKED BROWNIES WITH THEIR SOFT GOOEY CENTRES. SERVE WHILE WARM FROM THE OVEN OR LEAVE TO COOL COMPLETELY AND TOP WITH A SCOOP OF GOOD VANILLA ICE CREAM OR A SPOONFUL OF GREEK YOGURT FLAVOURED WITH A LITTLE GROUND CINNAMON AND HONEY. WHICHEVER WAY YOU CHOOSE THEY MAKE A FABULOUS FINALE TO A SUPPER SHARED WITH FRIENDS.

1 Preheat the oven to 140°C/275°F/Gas mark 1. Grease the inside of 6 individual china or foil dishes that are 10cm/4in in diameter and 4cm/1½in deep and set these on a baking sheet.

2 Put the butter, chocolate and caster sugar into a large heatproof bowl. Pour in the cream and set the bowl over a saucepan of gently simmering water, making sure that the water does not touch the base of the bowl. Heat for about 5 minutes, stirring gently from time to time, until the chocolate has completely melted and the mixture is smooth and glossy.

3 Take the bowl off the heat, and gradually stir in the egg yolks, one by one, until smooth. Whisk the egg whites in a separate bowl until a thick foam forms that very softly peaks when the whisk is lifted out of the mixture. Add to the chocolate and very gently fold together with a large metal or silicone spoon.

4 Spoon the chocolate mixture evenly into the dishes and bake for 16–18 minutes until the tops are dry to the touch, the mixture is set around the edges and the centre still has a soft slight wobble. Leave to stand for 10–15 minutes, then dust with sifted icing sugar, sprinkle with sliced pistachios and serve warm or cold. A scoop of salted cashew or vanilla ice cream on the side is also very good.

HALVA PARFAIT

6 large eggs, separated
115g/4oz caster sugar
400ml/14fl oz whipping cream
250g/9oz pack plain halva, sliced and broken into small pieces

fresh figs or sliced peaches, to serve (optional)

COULDN'T BE SIMPLER. IF YOU HAVEN'T BOUGHT HALVA BEFORE, IT IS MADE WITH TAHINI, SUGAR AND SOMETIMES VANILLA AND IS SOLD IN PACKS ABOUT THE SIZE OF A PACK OF BUTTER, EITHER PLAIN OR FLAVOURED WITH HONEY, PISTACHIOS OR CINNAMON. IT HAS A TEXTURE A LITTLE LIKE HONEYCOMB. ALTHOUGH YOU CAN SLICE IT, IT BREAKS AND CRUMBLES AS SOON AS YOU TOUCH IT WITH A KNIFE. SCRUNCH UP ANY BIGGER PIECES WITH YOUR FINGERS. UNLIKE OTHER HOMEMADE ICE CREAM, THIS IS EASY TO SLICE STRAIGHT FROM THE FREEZER. THANK YOU ANAT FOR GIVING US THIS RECIPE MANY YEARS AGO!

SERVES 6–8
PREP: 20 MINUTES
FREEZE: 6–8 HOURS,
OR OVERNIGHT

1 Put the egg whites and 2 teaspoons of the sugar into one large bowl and the egg yolks and the remaining sugar into another large bowl. Using an electric mixer, whisk the egg whites and sugar until thick moist-looking peaks that hold their shape when the whisk is lifted above the mixture form.

2 There's no need to wash the whisk – quickly use it to whisk the egg yolks and sugar together until very thick and pale, about 3–4 minutes. Now use the whisk to whip the cream in a smaller bowl until it forms soft swirls.

3 Fold the cream into the egg yolk mix, then fold in the crumbled halva. Gently fold in the egg whites until no white lumps remain. Pour the mixture into a 2.5 litre/4½ pint small roasting tin. If you don't have one that kind of size a disposable foil roasting dish, about 18 x 25 x 6cm/7 x 10 x 2½in works well, or use a large loaf tin or large plastic container. Cover with clingfilm or a lid and freeze for 6–8 hours, or overnight until firm.

4 Cut into thick slices to serve. It is delicious served on its own or with fresh figs or sliced peaches.

SERVES 6
PREP: 5 MINUTES
COOK: 55 MINUTES

ORANGE BLOSSOM RICE PUDDING

1 litre/1¾ pints water
200g/7oz risotto rice
500ml/18fl oz full-fat cold milk
140g/5oz granulated sugar
150ml/¼ pint double cream
½ tsp orange blossom water, plus
extra for sprinkling (optional)

To decorate:
chopped Turkish delight
chopped pistachios
plus a few sliced pistachios

RONEN: THIS IS MY SISTER'S RECIPE. FORGET ABOUT ENGLISH SCHOOL DINNER RICE PUDDING, THIS CREAMY SMOOTH VERSION IS MADE WITH RISOTTO RICE GENTLY COOKED ON THE HOB AND THEN FINISHED WITH DOUBLE CREAM, SUGAR AND JUST A HINT OF EXOTICALLY FRAGRANT ORANGE BLOSSOM WATER. IT'S LOVELY SERVED COLD DRIZZLED WITH A LITTLE EXTRA CREAM AND SPRINKLED WITH SOME CHOPPED TURKISH DELIGHT AND PISTACHIOS BUT JUST AS DELICIOUS SERVED AS SOON AS IT HAS BEEN MADE SPRINKLED WITH A LITTLE GROUND CINNAMON.

1 Pour the water into a saucepan, bring to the boil and then add the risotto rice. Bring the water back to the boil, then lower the heat and simmer gently for 15 minutes until the rice is beginning to soften and looks a little like porridge. Stir from time so that the rice doesn't stick to the pan.

2 Stir in the cold milk and bring to the boil, then lower the heat and simmer for about 40 minutes, stirring from time to time, until the rice is thick and creamy and nearly all the milk and water have been absorbed by the rice. Make sure to stir more often, the thicker the rice gets.

3 Add the sugar and cook over a low heat, stirring frequently, until the sugar has dissolved. Mix in the cream and cook for a further 5 minutes until the rice is soft. Stir in the orange flower water, then leave to cool slightly. Taste. If the orange flavour is too subtle, then you can add a little more orange blossom water.

4 Spoon into bowls or leave to cool completely. Serve, sprinkled with a little chopped Turkish delight, chopped and sliced pistachios and a little extra orange blossom water, if wished.

PANNA COTTA WITH ROSE WATER

5 leaves (7g/¼oz) gelatine
450ml/¾ pint double cream
150ml/¼ pint semi-skimmed milk
3 tbsp set honey
few drops of rose water, or to taste

To decorate:
tiny pale pink rose petals (optional)
chopped Turkish delight (optional)

SERVES 6
PREP: 15 MINUTES
SET: 4–5 HOURS

WE HAVE GIVEN THE CLASSIC ITALIAN DESSERT OUR VERY OWN MIDDLE EASTERN TWIST. JUST A DASH OF ROSE WATER ADDS AN EXOTIC PERFUME AND SERVED WITH PASTEL PINK ROSE PETALS MAKES THIS A LIGHT FINALE TO A SPECIAL MEAL.

1 Separate the gelatine sheets and put into a shallow bowl, just cover with cold water and leave to soak for 5 minutes.

2 Pour the cream and milk into a saucepan, add the honey and bring just to the boil, stirring until the honey has dissolved. Drain the water from the gelatine then add the softened sheets to the hot cream mixture, off the heat, and stir until they have dissolved.

3 Stir in a few drops of rose water, taste and add a few more drops, if liked. Pour the cream mixture into six 150 ml/ ¼ pint pudding moulds and leave to cool, then chill in the fridge for 4–5 hours until set.

4 To serve, leave the desserts in the moulds or turn out by dipping each mould into hot water for 10 seconds, loosen the top of the dessert with your fingertips, then invert on to a plate. Holding the mould and plate, jerk to release the panna cotta. Remove the moulds and decorate the desserts with a few tiny pink rose petals, if liked or chopped Turkish delight.

COOK'S TIP

ROSE WATER VARIES IN STRENGTH, SO ADD JUST A FEW DROPS, THEN TASTE AND ADD MORE IF NEEDED. YOU MIGHT ALSO LIKE TO TRY ADDING A LITTLE ROSE WATER TO SOME WHIPPED CREAM – GREAT WITH OUR CHOCOLATE BROWNIES (SEE P.120).

DRINKS

MINT & GINGER LEMONADE

150g/5½oz granulated sugar
150ml/¼ pint water
70g/2½oz piece fresh root ginger, scrubbed, there's no need to peel first, sliced

juice of 8 lemons

To serve:
chilled water and ice cubes
6 fresh mint sprigs
wafer-thin strips of fresh root ginger, cut with a vegetable peeler (optional)

EASY TO MAKE AND REALLY REFRESHING ON A HOT SUMMERY DAY, THIS DRINK IS GREAT FOR PARTIES, TOO. JUST SCALE UP THE QUANTITIES AND FOR THOSE WHO LIKE AN EXTRA HIT, TRY IT WITH A SPLASH OF WHITE RUM.

1 Put the sugar, water and ginger into a small saucepan and heat over a low heat, stirring until the sugar has dissolved. Bring to the boil, then take off the heat, cover with a lid or plate and leave to cool at room temperature for 2–3 hours for the flavours to develop.

2 Strain the lemon juice into a large measuring jug – you should have just over 400ml/ ¾ pint. Strain in the ginger syrup and stir to mix, then top up to 1.7 litres/3 pints with chilled water and ice cubes. Stir together, then pour into 6 glasses and add a mint sprig and strip of ginger, if using, to each to serve.

MAKES: 6 GLASSES
PREP: 10 MINUTES
COOK: 5 MINUTES
CHILL: 2–3 HOURS

HOT SPICED APPLE JUICE

2 tsp ground cinnamon
½ tsp grated nutmeg
¼ tsp ground cloves
¼ tsp ground ginger
1.25 litre bottle cloudy apple juice
4 cinnamon sticks, to serve (optional)

NOT EVERYONE IS A FAN OF TEA OR COFFEE AND THIS WARMING CAFFEINE-FREE DRINK WILL SOON HELP YOU TO THAW OUT ON A COLD WINTER'S DAY.

1 Mix all the ground spices together in a small bowl (make sure there are no lumps), then divide between 4 heavy heatproof glass tumblers.

2 Pour the apple juice into a saucepan and gently warm over a low heat, making sure that you don't boil it. Pour into the glasses and stir the juices and spices together with cinnamon sticks or teaspoons, if you prefer, and serve straight away.

MAKES 4 LARGE
TUMBLERS
PREP: 2 MINUTES
COOK: 2–3 MINUTES

CARDAMOM COFFEE

1 cardamom pod
225ml/8fl oz cold water
1–2 tsp granulated sugar, or to taste
1 tbsp finely ground coffee

WARM, FRAGRANT AND WONDERFULLY EXOTIC, TURKISH COFFEE WITH A TWIST, THIS IS TRADITIONALLY MADE IN AN IBRIK (BRIKI IN GREEK), A SMALL METAL JUG-LIKE SAUCEPAN WITH A LONG HANDLE. DON'T WORRY IF DON'T HAVE ONE, AS A SMALL SAUCEPAN WILL WORK JUST AS WELL. IT'S VITAL TO HAVE THE COFFEE GROUND VERY FINE UNTIL IT IS ALMOST LIKE POWDER. YOU CAN DO THIS AT HOME IN A SPICE MILL OR POWERFUL BLENDER OR ASK THE DELI TO GRIND THE COFFEE FOR 'TURKISH COFFEE'.

1 Put the cardamom pod in a mortar and crush with the pestle, then remove the seeds and grind them finely.

2 Pour the water into an ibrik or small saucepan, add enough sugar to taste, then heat until the sugar has dissolved. Bring just to the boil, then take off the heat and add the ground coffee, empty cardamom pod and the ground seeds.

3 Bring the water gently to the boil again, then take off the heat as soon as the coffee begins to foam. Leave to cool for 1–2 minutes, then put back on the heat and return to the boil so that the coffee is foaming. Pour into a coffee cup. Scoop out the cardamom pod, which will have floated to the surface, with a teaspoon. Leave to stand for 1–2 minutes for the coffee grounds to settle. Don't be tempted to stir the coffee or add milk or cream. Serve.

MAKES: 1 CUP
PREP AND COOK:
5 MINUTES

MINT & SAGE TEAS

30g/1oz fresh mint sprigs
850ml/1½ pints boiling water
sugar or honey, to taste (optional)

POPULAR SINCE ROMAN TIMES, MINT TEA IS STILL WIDELY DRUNK IN MIDDLE EASTERN CAFES AND HOMES. THE SCENT AND TASTE OF MINT IS THOUGHT TO IMPROVE A PERSON'S MOOD AND TO AID RELAXATION, WHILE ALSO ACTING AS A REFRESHING DIGESTIVE AND TUMMY SOOTHER.

Put the mint into a heatproof jug, pour over the boiling water, cover with a saucer and leave to brew for 4–5 minutes until the water is coloured pale green. Strain the tea into 4 heatproof glasses, then scoop out some of the mint from the jug and add a sprig to each glass. We prefer to serve it just as it is, but if you have a sweet tooth stir in a little sugar or honey to taste.

SAGE TEA

People have been cooking with sage since the fifth century BC. The Arabs used to associate it with immortality, while it's botanical name *Salvia* is from the Latin 'to save or to heal'. Herbalists used to have a saying 'Why should anyone die with sage in their garden'. While we cannot vouch for its lifesaving properties we do recommend it as a digestive, and as a soothing and calming caffeine-free pick-me-up. Make it in just the same way as mint tea and sweeten with a little honey, if liked.

MAKES: 4 GLASSES
PREP: 5 MINUTES

SACHLAV

3 tbsp cornflour
600ml/1 pint full-fat milk
150ml/¼ pint double cream
85g/3oz granulated sugar

To serve:
ground cinnamon
chopped peanuts and/or pistachios
coconut shavings

SERVES 4
PREP: 5 MINUTES
COOK: 4–5 MINUTES

TRADITIONALLY SERVED WARM FROM STREET VENDORS, THIS COMFORTING MILKY DRINK ALWAYS REMINDS US OF CHILDHOOD. DUST A GENEROUS AMOUNT OF GROUND CINNAMON OVER THE SURFACE WITH A SMALL TEA STRAINER, AND TOP WITH CHOPPED PEANUTS, PISTACHIOS AND COCONUT SHAVINGS. IF IT IS VERY THICK, IT CAN SOMETIMES BE HARD TO DRINK, SO IT IS WORTH GIVING GUESTS A SMALL TEASPOON WITH WHICH TO SCOOP IT UP.

1 Put the cornflour into a saucepan, mix in a little of the milk to make a smooth paste, then add the remaining milk, cream and sugar. Bring to the boil over a medium heat, stirring until slightly thickened.

2 As soon as the mixture has thickened, remove from the heat, pour into heatproof glasses and top with the ground cinnamon, chopped nuts and coconut shavings to serve.

NOTE

SACHLAV IS THE ARABIC AND HEBREW NAME FOR ORCHID AND THIS DRINK WAS ORIGINALLY THICKENED WITH GROUND ORCHID ROOT, ALTHOUGH CORNFLOUR, A MORE ACCESSIBLE EVERYDAY THICKENER, IS USED NOW.

OUZO & GRAPEFRUIT SLUSH

5 ruby grapefruits, freshly squeezed or 1 litre/1¾ pint carton chilled ruby grapefruit juice

125ml/4fl oz ouzo

4 tbsp chopped fresh mint

SERVES 4
PREP: 15 MINUTES
FREEZE: 3 HOURS

SLUSH PUPPIES FOR ADULTS! QUICK AND EASY TO MIX TOGETHER, THEN FREEZE IN A SHALLOW CONTAINER – THE LARGER THE TIN, THE THINNER THE MIXTURE WILL BE AND THE QUICKER IT WILL FREEZE. THE SECRET IS TO BREAK UP THE ICE WITH A FORK AT REGULAR INTERVALS SO THAT THE MIXTURE BECOMES LIKE FINE SNOW. SERVE IN SMALL GLASSES WITH A TEASPOON OR STRAWS. IF YOU ARE SQUEEZING YOUR OWN JUICE, KEEP THE GRAPEFRUIT SHELLS TO USE AS FUN SERVING DISHES.

1 Pour the grapefruit juice and ouzo into a large cake tin or roasting tin and mix together. Cover the top with clingfilm and put into the coldest part of the freezer. Freeze for 1 hour.

2 Take the tin out of the freezer and break up the ice with a fork. Return to the freezer and freeze for 2 hours, breaking up with a fork every 30–45 minutes until the mixture looks like fine snow.

3 Beat in the chopped mint and transfer to a plastic container, press a lid in place and freeze until needed. Break up with a fork just before serving scooped into grapefruit shells or glasses with little straws.

COOK'S TIP

YOU MIGHT ALSO LIKE TO TRY WITH ORANGE JUICE AND TEQUILA, FRESH LEMONADE AND GIN OR FROZEN CARDAMOM COFFEE VERSIONS.

QUICK SNACKS

HALVA COOKIES

100g/3½oz unsalted butter, at room temperature

85g/3oz caster sugar

85g/3oz tahini

½ tsp vanilla extract

1 tsp baking powder

150g/5½oz plain flour

THESE CRUMBLY SHORTBREAD–LIKE BISCUITS JUST MELT IN THE MOUTH. THEY TAKE ONLY A FEW MINUTES TO MAKE AND BAKE, BUT THE BAKING PROCESS IS CRITICAL, SO DON'T LEAVE THE KITCHEN WHILE THEY ARE BAKING, AS YOU NEED TO CATCH THEM WHEN THEY ARE LIGHT GOLDEN, NO MORE THAN THAT. IF YOU OVERCOOK THEM THEY WILL TAKE ON A SOUR, ALMOST BITTER, TASTE.

MAKES 15
PREP: 15 MINUTES
COOK: 8–10 MINUTES

1 Preheat the oven to 180°C/350°F/Gas mark 4 and line 2 baking trays with non-stick baking paper.

2 Cream the butter and sugar together in a bowl with a wooden spoon or beat in a food processor until light and fluffy.

3 Add the tahini and vanilla and beat together until smooth again. Add the baking powder and flour to another bowl and stir together, then gradually beat into the creamed tahini mix, pressing together with your hands to make a ball when it is too stiff to mix.

4 Scoop the dough into 15 mounds, then roll each one into a ball and put on the lined baking sheet, leaving a little space between them to spread during baking. Gently flatten the balls with a fork, then bake for 8–10 minutes until the tops have cracked and the biscuits are pale golden. Leave the cookies to cool and harden on the paper. If you eat them while they are still warm they will just crumble.

MORNING GRANOLA

250g/9oz medium oatmeal
55g/2oz pumpkin seeds
55g/2oz sunflower seeds
55g/2oz flaked almonds
40g/1½oz pistachio nuts, sliced
2 tbsp desiccated coconut
2 tbsp sesame seeds
4 tbsp vegetable oil
125ml/4fl oz (8 tbsp) date honey
1½ tsp ground cinnamon
pinch of sea salt
70g/2½oz dried cranberries
diced or sliced fruit and Greek yogurt
or milk, to serve

SERVES 6
MAKES: 650G/ILB 7OZ
PREP: 15 MINUTES
COOK: 30 MINUTES

DELICIOUSLY HEALTHY, THIS EASY BREAKFAST CEREAL IS NATURALLY SWEETENED WITH DATE HONEY, ALSO CALLED DATE SYRUP – IF YOU HAVEN'T USED IT BEFORE IT COMES IN JARS FROM THE HEALTH FOOD SHOP AND LOOKS A LITTLE LIKE TREACLE. THIS GRANOLA IS PACKED WITH OATMEAL FOR SLOW-RELEASE CARBS PLUS PROTEIN-RICH NUTS AND MINERAL-BOOSTING SEEDS TO POWER BOOST YOU UNTIL LUNCHTIME.

MAKE UP A BATCH OF THIS AT THE WEEKEND, AS YOU NEED TO BE IN THE KITCHEN TO STIR IT FREQUENTLY WHILE IT BAKES, THEN WHEN IT'S COLD PACK IT INTO A STORAGE JAR. FABULOUS SERVED WITH SLICED BANANAS, DICED PEACHES, OR WHATEVER FRUITS YOU HAVE AVAILABLE, PLUS A GENEROUS SPOONFUL OF GREEK YOGURT, OR KEEP IT REALLY SIMPLE AND JUST DRIZZLE WITH SOME MILK.

1 Preheat the oven to 150°C/300°F/Gas mark 2.

2 Put all the ingredients except the cranberries into a bowl and mix together with a spoon to evenly coat the oats, nuts and seeds with the oil and date syrup.

3 Tip into a large roasting tin and press into an even layer, then bake for 30 minutes, stirring every 5-10 minutes so that the mixture doesn't form large hard clumps. You will find that the granola in the corners will bake more quickly than that in the centre, so keep a careful eye on it while it bakes and remember to set the timer so that you don't forget to keep stirring.

4 When the granola is crisp and a deep brown, take out of the oven and leave to cool, stirring every now and again to keep it from making large clumps. When cold, stir in the cranberries, then store in a large jar, screw on the lid and keep in the fridge for up to a week. Serve with diced or sliced fruit and yogurt or milk.

TIP

IF YOU DON'T HAVE ALL THE NUTS OR ARE A LITTLE SHORT OF ONE INGREDIENT THEN MIX AND MATCH WITH WHAT YOU DO HAVE. PECANS OR MACADAMIA NUTS ALSO TASTE GREAT.

146 SALT-PICKLED CUCUMBERS

1kg/2¼lb fresh hard small cucumbers

5 garlic cloves

1–2 red chillies, split in half
(can also do a combination of
red and green chillies)

1 bunch of fresh dill

1 litre/1¾ pints water
(preferably mineral)

6 tsp coarse sea salt

2 tbsp white wine vinegar

2 bay leaves

pinch of black peppercorns

1 tbsp coriander seeds
or mustard seeds,
or cumin seeds

MAKES: 2 JARS
PREP: 20 MINUTES
COOK: 1–2 WEEKS

CHOOSE THE FRESHEST AND SMALLEST CUCUMBERS THAT YOU CAN FIND. WE USE MINI CUCUMBERS, WHICH ARE SOLD BY SOME RETAILERS (MOSTLY IMPORTED FROM JORDAN), AS THESE ARE THE BEST FOR PICKLING – THEY DON'T CONTAIN SO MUCH WATER AS THE LARGE/LONG CUCUMBERS THAT ARE SOLD IN THE SUPERMARKETS.

1 Wash the cucumbers thoroughly in cold water. Place them in a jar vertically, then put the garlic, chillies and dill in between the cucumbers so they all 'touch' each other.

2 The salt needs to dissolve in the water so the easiest way is to boil the water with the salt and vinegar and leave to cool. Then when you've left the water to cool to room temperature, add the bay leaves, peppercorns and coriander, mustard or cumin seeds. Add the water to the cucumbers, making sure that they are immersed in the water solution. If the jar you are using is not full, then add more salty water (1 litre/1¾ pints water to 5 teaspoons salt).

3 Close and seal the jar. In order to speed up the pickling process you can put the jar on the windowsill to catch the sunlight.

4 Taste the cucumbers every three days or so until they reach their required consistency. It should take between 1–2 weeks. Keep in the fridge once you're happy with the taste. It should keep for a month if not contaminated.

148 # PICKLED LEMONS

400g/14oz fresh hard lemons (about 4)
4 tbsp coarse sea salt
2 tbsp sunflower oil
½ roughly chopped green chilli and
½ roughly chopped red chilli
(optional)

THESE ARE SO VERSATILE. USE THEM FOR SALADS TO ADD ACIDITY, THEY'RE GREAT WITH GRILLED CHICKEN AND COMBINED WITH TAHINI SAUCE AND CHILLI, THEY MAKE A GOOD DIP. YOU CAN ALSO INCLUDE SOME CHILLIES TO ADD A BIT OF SPICE TO THE LEMONS (SEE PHOTO ON PAGE 147).

1 Slice the lemons into thin slices. Place on a large baking tray and sprinkle with the salt to make them 'sweat'. Leave them overnight, turning the slices once to make sure the salt reaches both sides.

2 Place the lemon slices, along with any liquid produced, in a clear glass Le Parfait-style clip jar and seal the lid. Leave for 2–3 days for the lemons to sweat some more.

3 Add the oil until the lemons are covered and add the chillies, if wished.

4 Close the jar and place in a dark dry place. Check the lemons every 2–3 days. They should be ready within 6–10 days and can last a few months.

MAKES: 1 JAR
PREP: 10 MINUTES
STAND: 9–13 DAYS

SPICED FAVA BEAN NIBBLES

250g/9oz dried fava beans or chickpeas, soaked overnight (or use canned, drained)

2 tsp bicarbonate of soda

dash of olive oil

2 tbsp dried oregano, plus extra for spinkling

sea salt and freshly ground pepper

2 tsp garlic powder (optional)

2 tsp chilli powder (optional)

THIS IS A CUTE AND FUN RECIPE THAT YOU CAN TRY WITH YOUR KIDS AT HOME. IT'S A PERFECT NIBBLE TO SERVE AT A FAMILY GATHERING. YOU CAN ALSO MAKE THIS WITH CHICKPEAS, BUT FAVA BEANS ARE MEATIER AND SOAK UP THE FLAVOURS BETTER. CHILDREN LIKE THESE WITH OREGANO, OR MAYBE A LITTLE GARLIC POWDER. ADULTS TEND TO PREFER SOMETHING A LITTLE SPICIER, SO OMIT THE OREGANO AND REPLACE WITH CHILLI POWDER.

1 Drain the soaked fava beans (or chickpeas) and place in a pan with enough water to cover by about 2cm and add the bicarbonate of soda. Bring to the boil, then turn down the heat and cook for 45 minutes until they're soft enough to squash between 2 fingers (but still have shape). Drain in a sieve and then pat dry with a kitchen paper (you want as little water as possible on the beans/peas).

2 In a mixing bowl, add the herbs and/or spices, the beans and the olive oil and mix well, taking care not to damage the beans. Season to taste.

3 Preheat the oven to 180°C/350°F/Gas mark 4. Spread the spiced beans over a baking tray lined with greaseproof paper and bake for 40 minutes. After 20 minutes take out the tray and give it a good shake to turn the beans. Return to the oven and repeat the process every 10 minutes. After 30 mins watch very carefully as they can burn easily. After about 40 minutes the beans will become brown and dry so take them out. When cool enough to taste, check they are nice and crunchy on the outside.

4 Serve in a deep bowl with a sprinkle of salt crystals and a little extra oregano to enhance the flavour. Great with beer or wine.

SERVES: 4–6
PREP: OVERNIGHT
SOAK (OPTIONAL)
COOK: 1½ HOURS

SOURDOUGH TOAST WITH RAW TAHINI & DATE HONEY

THIS ONE IS LESS OF A RECIPE AND MORE OF A SERVING SUGGESTION. RAW WHOLE TAHINI IS REALLY DELICIOUS WHEN SPREAD DIRECTLY FROM THE JAR OVER TOASTED SLICES OF SOURDOUGH BREAD. SIMPLY DRIZZLE WITH SOME DATE HONEY AND DEVOUR. IT MIGHT SEEM A LITTLE 'HARDCORE' FOR THOSE NOT BROUGHT UP ON THE TASTE OF TAHINI, BUT EVERYONE WE'VE EVER SERVED THIS TO HAS LOVED IT.

RONEN: THIS IS MY DAD'S MAIN CONTRIBUTION TO THE HUMMUS BROS. RECIPE PORTFOLIO. TRULY HIS CREATION, ITS A SORT OF DISASSOCIATED HALVA WITH A TWIST. HE'S NOT EXACTLY A CHEF BUT I CAN'T TAKE THIS ONE FROM HIM!

HUMMUS BROS

FREE-FROM LIST	GLUTEN-FREE	LACTOSE-FREE	NUT-FREE
Hummus Recipe	✓	✓	✓
TOPPINGS			
Hummus w/ Slow-cooked Chickpeas	✓	✓	✓
Hummus w/ Mushrooms	✓	✓	✓
Hummus w/ Chicken	✓	✓	✓
Hummus w/ Chunky Beef	✓	✓	✓
Hummus w/ Lamb & Pine Nuts	✓	✗	✗
Hummus w/ Lamb Rogan Josh	✓	✗	✓
Hummus w/ Chilli con Carne	✓	✓	✓
Hummus w/ Mexican Beef	✓	✗	✓
Hummus w/ Moroccan Meatballs	✗	✓	✓
Masabacha	✓	✓	✓
Hummus w/ Fava Beans	✓	✓	✓
Shakshuka	✓	✓	✓
Hummus w/ Spicy Sausage & 3 Pepper Stew	✓	✓	✓
Hummus w/ Chicken Tikka Masala	✓	✗	✗
FALAFEL			
Green Falafel	✓	✓	✓
Sweet Potato Falafel	✓	✓	✓
Spicy Red Falafel	✓	✓	✓
Mixed Bean Falafel	✓	✓	✓
WRAPS			
Falafel Wrap	✗	✗	✓
Sabich: Aubergine & Egg Wrap	✗	✓	✓
Beef Wrap	✗	✓	✓
SOUPS			
Chickpea & Chorizo Soup	✓	✓	✓
Tomato soup w/ Pitta Bread Croutons	✗	✓	✓
Tomato soup w/out Pitta Bread Croutons	✓	✓	✓
Spicy Lentil Soup	✓	✓	✓
Mixed Bean & Bacon Soup	✗	✓	✓
Jerusalem Artichoke Soup with Chestnut Cream	✓	✗	✗
SALADS			
Roasted Aubergine Salad	✓	✓	✓
Roasted Vegetable Salad	✓	✓	✓

	GLUTEN-FREE	LACTOSE-FREE	NUT-FREE	155
Tabouleh	✗	✓	✓	
Mixed Vegetable Salad	✓	✓	✓	
Falafel Salad	✓	✗	✓	
Greek Salad	✓	✗	✓	
Fatoush	✗	✓	✓	
Cauliflower w/ Green Tahini	✓	✓	✓	

BREADS AND SAUCES

	GLUTEN-FREE	LACTOSE-FREE	NUT-FREE
Tahini Sauce	✓	✓	✓
Green Tahini Sauce	✓	✓	✓
Guacamole	✓	✓	✓
Tzatziki	✓	✗	✓
Tomato & Coriander Salsa	✓	✓	✓
Green Chilli Sauce	✓	✓	✓
Yellow Sauce	✓	✓	✓
Garlic & Lemon Sauce	✓	✓	✓
Wholemeal Pitta Bread	✗	✓	✓
Flatbread w/ Za'atar	✗	✓	✓
Labaneh (Sour Yogurt Cheese)	✓	✗	✓

DESSERTS

	GLUTEN-FREE	LACTOSE-FREE	NUT-FREE
Malabi	✓	✗	✓
Chocolate Brownies	✓	✗	✓
Halva Parfait	✓	✗	✓
Orange Blossom Rice Pudding	✓	✗	✓
Panna Cotta w/ Rose Water	✓	✗	✓

DRINKS

	GLUTEN-FREE	LACTOSE-FREE	NUT-FREE
Mint & Ginger Lemonade	✓	✓	✓
Hot Spiced Apple Juice	✓	✓	✓
Cardamom Coffee	✓	✓	✓
Mint & Sage Teas	✓	✓	✓
Sachlav	✓	✗	✗
Ouzo & Grapefruit Slush	✓	✓	✓

QUICK SNACKS

	GLUTEN-FREE	LACTOSE-FREE	NUT-FREE
Halva Cookies	✗	✗	✓
Morning Granola	✗	✓ (unless served with milk or yogurt)	✗
Salt-Pickled Cucumbers	✓	✓	✓
Pickled Lemons	✓	✓	✓
Spiced Fava Bean Nibbles	✓	✓	✓

INDEX

Page numbers in **bold** denote
an illustration

ACKNOWLEDGEMENTS

HUMMUS BROS. WOULD NOT BE WITHOUT THE SUPPORT AND DEDICATION OF THE FOLLOWING PEOPLE.

Noam Givon, who has been with us from Day One. Artur Kaczmarczyk, for making all the wonderful food we serve each day. Fred Edwards, who believed in us from the first meeting. Varun Khanna, our unofficial chairman emeritus, for putting his money where his mouth is. Ivo Slezak and Artur Karasiewicz, for sticking with us and giving 100%. Ryan Matzner, our original marketing genius, and Eran Hovav, who helped set everything up at first.

Arik, Roy Glanfield and Carl Smith, for always supplying us with the best ingredients. Tim Chakera and Philip Otvos, whose work and opinions have been invaluable for the last nine years.

Roly Grant and Phil Koh at Buro Creative, for helping us convince our customers. Martin Chamberlain and Benjamin Davis, for supporting our initial growth.

Thank you to Karen Thomas for the beautiful photos, Sara Lewis for home economy, food styling (and importantly for developing the recipes to be suitable for home cooks!), Wei Tang for props, Laura Russell and Emma Wicks for book design, Kathy Steer for the copy editing, Kom Patel for marketing and Simon Ballard for our portrait picture. A special thanks to Emily Preece-Morrison for producing this book from start to finish.

Thanks to George Grylls for being such a loyal fan and helping this book happen.

Thank you to Hannah and Orat for ten years of developing and testing recipes.

Finally, we'd like to dedicate this book to our families who have encouraged us every step of the way.

Christian Mouysset & Ronen Givon
The Hummus Brothers

Branch locations
Soho – 88 Wardour St., London W1F 0TJ
Holborn – Victoria House, 37-63 Southampton Row, London WC1B 4DA
St Paul's – 128 Cheapside, London EC2V 6BT
Exmouth Market – 62 Exmouth Market, London EC1R 4QE

For more information, visit:
www.hbros.co.uk
facebook.com/hbros
twitter.com/hbros

160

First published in the United Kingdom in 2014 by

Pavilion Books Company Ltd

1 Gower Street

London WC1E 6HD

ISBN: 978-1-90910-898-1

A CIP catalogue record for this book is available from the British Library

10 9 8 7 6 5 4 3 2 1

Reproduction by Mission, Hong Kong

Printed by 1010 Printing International Ltd, China

This book can be ordered direct from the publisher at www.pavilionbooks.com

Commissioning editor: Emily Preece-Morrison

Design and layout: Laura Russell and Emma Wicks

Home economist and recipe developer: Sara Lewis

Photographer: Karen Thomas, except image on p.7 by Simon Ballard